# A QUESTION OF TIME

*Angela Molnos*

# A QUESTION OF TIME

## Essentials of
## Brief Dynamic Psychotherapy

*Angela Molnos*

Foreword by
*Dennis Brown*

London
**KARNAC BOOKS**

First published in English in 1995 by
H. Karnac (Books) Ltd.
58 Gloucester Road
London SW7 4QY

**British Library Cataloguing in Publication Data**

Molnos, Angela
   A Question of Time: Essentials of Brief Dynamic Therapy
   I. Title
   616.8914

   ISBN 1 85575 107 0

Printed in Great Britain by BPC Wheatons Ltd, Exeter

# CONTENTS

# LIST OF FIGURES

# ABOUT THE AUTHOR

ANGELA MOLNOS was born in Budapest, Hungary, in 1923. She fought in the Italian underground during the war, and she studied modern linguistics, philosophy, and psychology in Bologna, Padua, and at the Free University of Berlin. She obtained her doctorate in psychology. Her main interest in the 1950s was the study of national stereotypes and prejudices. On behalf of the Ifo-Institute for Economic Research (Munich) and later as a Ford Foundation Project Specialist, she conducted social psychological research in East Africa during the 1960s. In 1973 she came to live in London, where she studied brief dynamic psychotherapy and qualified as a group analyst. She is best known for her work in brief dynamic psychotherapy, for devising the visual aid of the four triangles to represent its process, and for her clear and concise formulations.

Her publications include several books: *Die sozialwissenschaftliche Erforschung Ostafrikas* (Berlin: Springer-Verlag, 1965); *Attitudes towards Family Planning in East Africa* (Munich: Weltforum Verlag, 1968); *Cultural Source Materials for Population Planning in East Africa* (in four volumes; Nairobi:

East African Publishing House, 1972-1973); *Our Responses to a Deadly Virus* (London: Karnac Books for The Institute of Group Analysis and The Group-Analytic Society, 1990); *Waiting on Wonder* (London: Circle Press Publications, 1992). Seminal articles of hers have been published in several languages and appeared in German, French, Spanish, American, and English scientific journals, such as the *Kölner Zeitschrift für Soziologie und Sozialpsychologie; Revue de Psychologie des Peuples; Clínica y Análisis Grupal, Revista de psicoterapia y psicología aplicada; International Journal of Short-term Psychotherapy; British Journal of Psychotherapy;* and *Group Analysis, the Journal of Group-Analytic Psychotherapy.*

# FOREWORD

## Dennis Brown

Angela Molnos has written a challenging book. Her writing has always been perceptive and original. Her personal and professional development have taken surprising turns, as will be known to those who have followed her writing and as will be seen in the brief notes about the author. At each turn Dr Molnos has brought acute intelligence to bear from a viewpoint that has not been misted by conventional groundedness in a familiar setting. She has kept moving intellectually, and her own observations and insights provide us with antidotes to complacency and overfamiliarity. Throughout, she has demonstrated a tenacious honesty and a great capacity to stay true to her principles. She has done this while struggling to understand new ways of helping in further critical areas of human suffering and need. This book is an excellent example of her work, and a very timely one.

Analytical psychotherapy itself is in something of a crisis, beset by publicized doubts about its efficacy in this Age of Accountancy, challenges by the myriad alternative forms of therapy, and even reports of abuse of patients by psychotherapists. While these threats are largely, in my view, unfounded, they provide a challenge that can be beneficial to analytical psychotherapy. What Angela Molnos provides is a challenge from within, following the tradition of Ferenczi, Alexander and French, Balint, Malan, and others.

What is original about her work is the way in which the developing thread of Dr Molnos' intellectual interest in disparate areas is woven into a powerful argument that challenges prejudice and the collusive avoidance of the truth of human suffering. Hers is a deeply analytic, psychodynamic approach. She describes and explains tellingly the bias against brief dynamic psychotherapy, at the same time stressing the importance of actively challenging resistance and working through the transference. Dr Molnos describes well the committed and engaged attitude required of the therapist. The clinical examples are short but compelling. She stresses the importance of using anger in a positive way, even from the first session—an ability that characterizes what she calls "The Relentless Healer". But for brief dynamic psychotherapy to be effective, Dr Molnos insists that confrontation has to be simultaneously balanced by holding even from the start.

Angela Molnos describes her own concept of "destructive idealization" in which splitting conceals its ultimate destructiveness, which she found so clearly in her studies with staff working with AIDS sufferers. She makes plain that the danger of idealization is related to that of fundamentalism and Utopianism in the religious and political spheres. In psychotherapy, particularly long-term psychotherapy that keeps postponing separation and avoiding the reality of time, the equivalent danger is that of aiming for illusory perfection. A "perfect" analysis is sometimes needed by the analyst rather than by the patient.

In my view, all psychotherapists will benefit from reading this short book. This includes those non-analytical psychotherapists with a superficially optimistic view of brief work, and perhaps particularly those analytical psychotherapists "addicted" to long-term work, whether individual or group. There *is* a risk in timelessness in psychoanalysis and group analysis. There *is* risk also in being too passive—especially when it colludes with avoiding painful and hateful feelings. Challenging resistances can be left too late. Search for perfection can be a self-indulgence of the therapist that is *not* in the patient's interest.

I find myself sharply reminded of these truths on reading this book, which led me to reflect on those "pure" psychoanalysts for whom "truth" is more important than "curing" the patient. True to Angela Molnos' sense of style, this book about brief dynamic psychotherapy is itself brief. But it is full of clinical meat and academic pungency. It keeps you engaged and working hard, as in effective brief dynamic psychotherapy. I believe that there are few psychotherapists of any persuasion who will not be stimulated and changed by reading it.

# INTRODUCTION

T his small volume is based on talks I gave in 1993 and 1994. The decision to publish them in this format was made partly because of the many requests for copies of the talks and also because the four sections belong quite naturally together. They deal with questions central to the theory and practice of brief dynamic psychotherapy I have been exploring on and off for over half a century, but especially during the last fifteen years or so: our experience and conceptualization of time, shortening techniques in analytic psychotherapies, the role of anger in everyday life and in the therapeutic relationship, and the need to formulate the aims of analytic psychotherapies. Also reflected between the lines is my keen interest in the social, cultural, and language problems of our times.

When I first went to university in the 1940s and read Cesare Musatti's two authoritative volumes on psychoanalysis, I immediately became fascinated by the subject. One major doubt, however, presented itself there and then. Why does it have to take so long? My question was answered many years later when I started to attend David H.

Malan's Brief Psychotherapy Seminar at the Tavistock Clinic in London, had patients under his supervision, and became acquainted with H. Davanloo's approach and that of many others working in the field of brief dynamic psychotherapy. Group-analytic training helped to clarify that question too. The answer to it lies in many lengthening factors, but, of course, the question itself is redundant because in most cases it does not need to take so long.

Although this volume deals with brief dynamic psycho-therapy for individuals, many references are made to short-term group analysis too as a reminder that often the principles of individual therapy apply to group therapy as well.

The main aim of this book is to dispel some termin-ological, conceptual, and ideological confusion around the purpose of psychotherapy, the time spent in it, and the rationale for shortening analytic therapies. New ideas are introduced not to add to existing ones, but in an attempt to place some prevalent ambiguities and misunderstandings in their proper context. Basic concepts expressed through terms such as "boundaries", "transference", "short-term", "brief", "analytic", "dynamic" are elucidated.

It is hoped that this book might be read not only by practitioners exploring fairly controversial territory, but also by students and novice analytic psychotherapists and counsellors. Anyone interested in brief dynamic psycho-therapy might find it helpful.

Each chapter is self-contained. Where it has seemed in-appropriate to repeat a line of thought already dealt with, a reference to its appearance in another chapter is provided. Nevertheless, a few repetitions occur in order to spare the reader having to look up too many cross-references in the volume.

For simplicity's sake, I use the masculine pronouns (he, him, his) for a patient or group member whenever I am not talking specifically about a female patient. The neutral pro-nouns (it, its) are used for a baby or young child of either sex. The feminine pronouns (she, her, hers) are used for the therapist or the group conductor throughout the text.

The figures are designed to double as handouts or to be copied as overhead projector transparencies for teaching purposes.

Finally, I would like to thank most warmly all those who encouraged me and helped in a variety of ways to create this volume. First of all, Dr Patricia Morris, who gave me invaluable editorial advice and proposed the main title; Sarah T. Willis, who contributed with painstakingly accurate criticism throughout; Dr Dorothy M. Edwards, who made some brilliant suggestions concerning the second chapter; Ewa Gottesman and Cynthia Rogers, who worked closely with me in two of the workshops; the Group-Analytic Society (London) and its president, Bryan Boswood, for giving me the go-ahead to convene the Society's 22nd London Workshop; and Robert Gottesman and Isobel Conlon, the organizers of the workshops in Portsmouth and in Leeds, respectively. I am grateful to the participants of all three events for their perspicacious questions, which helped me to focus on the kind of information and debate so needed now in the field of brief analytic psychotherapies.

London, February 1995

# A QUESTION OF TIME

# CHAPTER ONE

# Time in our times
# and time in psychotherapy

I n this chapter some ideas are explored about the ways
in which we perceive time in daily life and in psychotherapy. In it, the stark contrast between two facts is
shown: one is that we live at an ever faster pace, and the
other is that the pace of psychotherapies tends to be slowing
down. Unless we actively do something about it, analytic
therapies become longer.

The thesis proposed is that time itself—its unconscious
suspension, our unconscious experience of it—is the principal lengthening factor in analytic psychotherapies. It is
the magic lure of timelessness hovering over all analytic
psychotherapies that makes termination of therapy so hard.
Timelessness takes us away from our terror of finite time,

This chapter is based on the keynote talks I gave at the 22nd London
Workshop of the Group-Analytic Society (London), December 1993, and
the 9th Northern Summer Workshop of the Yorkshire Association for
Psychodynamic Psychotherapy, held in Leeds, June 1994. I convened
both workshops under the title: "Being together briefly: an exploration
of short-term approaches within the group-analytic framework".

our terror of endings, and, ultimately, our terror of death. We find comfort in the rhythms emerging from the therapeutic time-patterns, the recurrence of the sessions. The time dimension affects all of us, the therapist no less than the patient. Some aspects of the time dimension and the implications for psychotherapy are explored in this chapter.

## Conceptualization of time and sense of time

Before talking about our fear of time, let us see how we conceptualize time and how we actually experience time. Conceptualization of time and sense of time are not one and the same.

We tend to conceptualize time as something absolute, that is to say, categorical, universal, fixed, and measurable. We measure it by the clock and the calendar. Time is ever-present—it always accompanies us, and it goes on forever, completely unaffected by anything else. Kronos is supreme, the father of all Gods. We visualize time mostly as a line, a ribbon, a road, or a river that stretches or flows from the past into the future, with distinct markers on it signposting segments all the way along. We progress on it from one signpost to the next.

Although this conceptualization is consonant with our life-style and works well on the whole, there are experiences that challenge it head-on. Arriving at Kennedy Airport and being confronted for the first time with the five-hour difference between London and New York or the realization of having lost a whole calendar day after crossing the International Date Line in the Pacific can shake anyone's idea of absolute time. The appearance of the repressed during the therapy hour might also challenge the notion of linear time. It might be so vivid as to make us feel that the past itself has returned and is no longer behind us, but here with us.

## How does the sense of time develop?

Our sense of time develops and grows along with consciousness (Hartocollis, 1986, p. 5). The child acquires a sense of
time step by step as it emerges from the primordial symbiotic union, discovers the distinction between its mother and
itself, its body, and its surroundings, and begins to come to
grips with realities beyond and within its reach. The delays
in getting its needs met awaken in the child a sense of time
as well as a sense of reality. "The first intuition of duration
appears as an interval which stands between the child and
the fulfilment of its desires" (Whitrow, 1988, p. 5). Delay in
the fulfilment of its wishes is also responsible for the child's
ability to distinguish between present, future, and past—in
that order. "Up to the age of 18 months or more children
appear to live only in the present. . . . Between then and 30
months, they tend to acquire a few words relating to the
future, such as 'soon', but almost none that concerns the
past . . . the use of 'tomorrow' precedes that of 'yesterday',
. . . " (Whitrow, 1988, p. 6).

How the mother and other care-givers negotiate the infant's need fulfilment and the temporary deprivations
between the experience of need and its fulfilment will have a
profound effect on the person's emotional development, as
well as on his or her sense of time. The two will stay closely
linked. The perception and handling of real time in later life
will remain loaded with the early nurturing experiences and
fantasies from the past.

A person's attitude towards time can be equated with his
attitude towards authority figures. If the infant has experienced arbitrary and excessively critical authority figures, a
dismissive attitude towards time may result. Neurotic "killing time" is aggression against the parent (DuBois, 1954;
Wiggins, 1983, p. 63). Patients who use the so-called "narra-
tive defence" are killing therapeutic time. In group therapy
even the group-as-a-whole might be engaged in it.

We know how difficult it is for some patients to keep to
the therapeutic time boundaries, how they loathe them as

an expression of the therapist's clinical coldness and indifference. For them, the time boundaries symbolize the mother's rigid and unreasonable refusal to feed on demand. If the therapy progresses well, the same time boundaries will be perceived for what they are meant to be: the invisible walls of a safe space in which the individual or the group can hold together and be held together in order to develop.

## Time in childhood

Our sense of time changes dramatically during our lives. As we grow older, time, as indicated by the clock and the calendar, appears to rush by faster and faster.

Everyone seems to remember how slowly time used to pass in childhood. A day was a long time, a week almost eternity, and beyond that a month, a year the never-never land. The agony of waiting for one's desires or expectations to be fulfilled was hard to bear. This intense, impatient longing for the future occurs whenever the child's basic experience of blissful, timeless, eternal present is disrupted.

No endings or death seem to exist in the childhood experience of timeless paradise (Bonaparte, 1940). The oceanic feeling of limitless contentment, of timelessness can be explained as a fantasy (or memory?) ". . . in which mother and child are endlessly united" (Bergler & Roheim, 1946, p. 190).

The disruption comes in the form of a parental demand, harsh words, physical pain, illness, an accident, loss of a loved object, and so on. The child wishes for the hurt, the pain, to go away and something else to come in its place: a good word from mum or dad, a miracle cure, a new pet. The wish to become older, to become an adult, is awakened. Images of a lost paradise are projected into the future. The child's attention switches to the future and to time itself. That is when time seems to move at a snail's pace.

## Duration

Our sense of time, including our sense of duration, depends not only on our age, but also on our physical condition and mental state. They, in their turn, can be influenced by alcohol, drugs, sensory deprivation, and many other factors.

Whether a given period of time appears to be long or short will depend on where our attention is focused. The more attention we pay to time itself, as measured by clocks and calendars, the longer the same unit of time seems to last, and vice versa. Never is a minute so long as when we focus our attention on the second hand going round and round the face of our watch or on the succession of 60 numbers displacing each other on a digital clock.

A group therapy session in which a great deal has been happening often ends with remarks like: "Is it time already? I thought we had just started!" In such instances the group-as-a-whole has been intently concentrating on some issue other than time. There are other sessions in which an oceanic feeling of complete harmony, trust, and relaxation prevails and which also finish with the regret that it was over too soon. The latter is the experience of symbiotic union that touches on a sense of eternity and timelessness and bypasses real time. Furthermore, in a therapy group the time experience of the same session might be different for different members—"too short" for some, "too long" for others.

A therapy group or an individual patient who is stuck finds that time does not pass. There are furtive glances at watches or the clock. The attention is becoming focused on real time. There is frustration, unexpressed anger with the therapist. "Why does she not help us to find out what is wrong? I wish she would say something." In a brief, time-limited therapy, be it individual or group, such blockages will be addressed immediately.

The relativity of duration can be observed and experienced through the way in which we relate to time near the end of a given interval. There is an increase in awareness of time when a given interval is about to terminate (Wiggins,

1983, p. 63–64). Many patients seem to react strongly to the last few minutes of the session. Some try to extend them, others to shorten them. Often very significant material is produced in the final minutes. At the end of a long-term therapy, once the termination date has been fixed, work is likely to intensify.

## Cultural relativity of time

Another proof of the relativity of time, if we need one, lies in the great cultural differences in how we conceptualize and experience time. It is through the vehicle of the mother tongue that the child learns and develops concepts. They are the product of the culture into which the child is born and in which it is brought up. So, too, are ideas about time.

The Sioux Indians have no word for "late" or for "waiting". The Sioux speaker who has not learned any other language does not know what it is to wait or to be late (Hall, 1959, p. 25). The Nuer of Sudan ". . . have no equivalent of our word 'time'". The language of the Hopi of Arizona "contains no words, grammatical forms, constructions, or expressions that refer to time or any of its aspects. . . . its verbs have no tenses" (Whitrow, 1988, pp. 8–9).

To conclude what has been said so far, I want to emphasize once more that so-called real time is a mental and cultural construct, that ". . . there is no unique intuition of time that is common to all mankind . . . " (Whitrow, 1988, p. 10). Our ideas of space and time are mental constructs, and as such they have to be learned (p. 186).

## Time's arrow and time's cycle

To approach the question of why and how time is a frightening issue, we first have to distinguish between time's arrow and time's cycle. I mentioned earlier that we tend to view

time as a road, a ribbon, a straight line, or a river coming
from the past, passing through the present and stretching
into the future. This imagery represents a particular mental
construct of time, namely the linear concept of time. It is
also called time's arrow. As we will see further on, by itself it
is the most frightening concept of time.

Time's arrow implies that every moment is unique, that
". . . history is an irreversible sequence of unrepeatable
events" and that all ". . . moments, considered in proper
sequence, tell a story of linked events moving in a direction"
(Gould, 1988, pp. 10–11). For us Western Europeans of the
twentieth century, with our linear way of looking at history,
it is difficult to imagine any other ways of conceptualizing
time.

Yet, there is another mental construct of time, which is
completely different. It is called time's cycle. According to
this construct of time, "Fundamental states are immanent
in time, always present and never changing. Apparent
motions are parts of repeating cycles, . . . time has no direction" (Gould, 1988, p. 11). Most people throughout history
held fast to time's cycle and have viewed time's arrow as
either unintelligible or too frightening to contemplate. "Interest in the 'irreversible' and the 'new' in history is a recent
discovery in the life of humanity" (Eliade, 1954, p. 48).

## Western culture under the terror of time's arrow

Contemporary Western culture has developed and exists as
a function of time's arrow. It is a prerequisite for our understanding of events. Without this linear concept of time, it
would be difficult to conceive of the idea of progress or
biological evolution (Morris, 1984, p. 11). "The clock has
been at the center of Western technology since its invention
in the Middle Ages . . . " (Bolter, 1984, p. 101).

Time's arrow is linear time—one-directional, irreversible,
what we consider "real" time. It implies the uniqueness of
every day, of every moment of the day. They all pass one

after the other and disappear for good. It is a frightening concept because it carries the inevitability of change. Our old diaries, which had served us well to plan ahead, become the concrete reminder of times gone forever, of separation anxiety and pain about loss (Bergler & Roheim, 1946, p. 190). Ultimately, the horror of time, which resides in all humans (Bonaparte, 1940), is linked to the fear of destruction and death (Hartocollis, 1986, p. 227).

In the last thirty years or so, we have been experiencing an unprecedented acceleration of linear time. The mediaeval clock has been joined by the twentieth-century computer. The microchip revolution has produced mind-boggling changes in daily living. Fast means of transport, the gathering and dissemination of information, live images from around the globe and beyond on the screens in our homes have altered our experience of time and space.

Not only has the world shrunk, but time itself seems to get shattered and fragmented at every step. Life is governed by time-schedules. We have become increasingly time-conscious, time-obsessed. We worry more about time itself than about what we actually do. "We no longer measure profound social change in generations, but rather by the decade or less." (Mann, 1973b, pp. 8–9). Who can reconjure the emotions surrounding the Berlin Wall? Who can remember the times when Gorazde, Gornji Vakuf, Tuzla, Vukovar, Banja Luka, Srebrnica were foreign place names, devoid of meaning, Dubrovnic just an attractive holiday resort, and Sarajevo a strange-sounding town with a resonance from the First World War? Who can remember the times when we all knew for certain that genocide would never again be repeated on European soil, when its obscene synonym, "ethnic cleansing", had not yet soiled our daily language? Since I first wrote these lines, more names have emerged from blissful obscurity. The Tutsi and the Hutu tribes in Rwanda are crying out for help. Genocide is now talked about every day. Things change faster than we can comprehend what is happening (Mann, 1973b, p. 9).

Thus, not only is time's arrow—a terrifying concept in itself—deeply ingrained in our brains and our lives, but we also experience its continual acceleration. In today's Western metronomic, microchip society, we are stressed by an excess of activity as well as by the ever-present and intensifying terror of linear time. We are frightened and look for escape routes.

The civilized, leisurely ways of suspending our awareness of time's passage—sleep, dreams, daydreams, holidays, a drink on the way home—don't seem to work any longer. The search for escape routes from accelerating linear time becomes intense. People turn to heavy drinking, drugs, meditation, esoteric beliefs and practices. Others try to defeat linear time by working around the clock and organizing life perfectly so as to feel they have time under their control. Such an illusion becomes increasingly difficult to sustain.

As time rushes by ever faster, the anxiety increases. We become more and more anxious about time and personal death. To soothe the anxiety, we demand instant gratifications and instant cures. Our own ". . . death becomes increasingly unacceptable. We ask medicine to eliminate death itself" (Mann, 1973b, p. 9). Given this high level of anxiety, the question arises: what is it exactly that patients and practitioners are asking psychotherapy to do?

### Time in psychotherapy: prejudices against brief dynamic psychotherapy

Strangely enough, we do not seem to expect instant cures from psychotherapy. On the contrary, patients and therapists alike tend to believe that the longer an analytic psychotherapy takes, the better it is, that the more weekly sessions, the "deeper", the more "intensive" the process will be, that except for holiday and weekend breaks, there should be no interruptions, and that once the therapy is terminated, the "cure" will be complete and the patient will never again need therapy. The few patients who ask for brief therapy more often than not just want to get it over with quickly and avoid the pain of change. The few therapists

who practise brief dynamic psychotherapy (BDP) in this
country do not feel entirely at ease with it.

The prejudices against any form of brief, time-limited
analytic psychotherapy are wide-spread. At best, it is considered insufficient, superficial therapy or helpful only to
those who are healthy. On the part of health workers who
deal with mentally disturbed patients, also, there can be
many objections to forms of brief therapy. These objections
are mostly borne out of misunderstandings and lack of any
first-hand knowledge or experience of brief dynamic psychotherapy.

The following are doubts and objections to brief dynamic
psychotherapy expressed by a mixed group of personnel in a
hospital:

> It is immoral, a "con". . . . It is a new fad. . . . It brings
> about superficial changes only. . . . The changes in the
> patient are short-lived. . . . It is just "wallpapering" over
> the cracks. . . . It is tantalizing for the patient. . . .
> There is insufficient time to learn to trust the therapist.
> . . . In the hospital we are forced to offer brief treatment
> and unable to work at a deeper level. . . . The adult
> psyche is too complex for brief therapy. . . . The time is
> insufficient for working through. . . . The therapist is
> aggressive. . . . Brief dynamic psychotherapy teaches
> the patient to be aggressive. . . . It is harmful to the
> patient . . . Only "healthy" people are selected for brief
> dynamic psychotherapy. . . . It is too difficult to learn.
> . . . It goes against our training.

Except for the last of these objections, none is actually
valid.

More serious is, of course, the resistance of the learned,
analytically trained psychotherapy establishment. To practise brief forms of dynamic psychotherapy means to have to
go against the grain, to have to withstand the invisible yet
solid social pressure exerted by colleagues. This social pressure persists even though much of what theoreticians and
practitioners of brief dynamic psychotherapy advocate is
". . . what long term therapists' common sense has been
telling them for years". The basic principles articulated by

brief dynamic psychotherapy are the same as those all good therapists follow. Some do so with a feeling of guilt, which accounts ". . . for why therapists do all those things they'd never tell their supervisors (who also secretly do them, without letting on to their supervisees)" (Wachtel, 1988, p. viii).

I can think of no more than three types of circumstances in which an analytically trained psychotherapist may practise brief psychotherapy without losing status. One case is when a well-motivated patient comes with his own ready-made termination date. For instance, he wants to sort out a problem before leaving this country for good in three months' time. The non-negotiable time-limit, the focus on a central problem, and the patient's determination to do something about it, offer the best starting-point for effective brief therapy. Most psychotherapists who do long-term work have one or more such success stories to tell. However, these cases are usually recounted only as interesting anecdotes, curious deviations from the prevalent norm of long-term work.

Another such circumstance is that of the psychotherapist who practices within the constraints of public-sector health care. The therapist's status remains safe as long as she agrees with the general opinion that it would be so much better to do long-term work "if only we had the resources". Thus, a lot of excellent brief work done within public-sector health care tends to be devalued as therapy on the hop and on the cheap.

Finally, there are psychotherapists of such high standing and international renown that their status cannot be diminished even if they advocate and practise brief psychotherapy.

Directly associated with the prejudice of "the longer the better" is the concomitant idea that once psychotherapy is terminated, the person should be able to live happily ever after without needing help again (Budman, 1981b, p. 465). This idea is not based on experience or common sense. In fact, the offer of intermittent or recurrent assistance is the norm in most helping professions. It is also practised in couple and family therapy.

A third prejudice considers individual analytic therapy to be essentially superior to all forms of group treatment. Among group analysts there might even be a trend to give up groups progressively and to do increasingly more individual work (Grotjahn, 1983, p. 258).

The resistance against each of the three—time-limited therapy, intermittent or recurrent therapy, and group therapy—is strong. The resistance against a combination of all three is even stronger.

## A history of resistance to shortening psychoanalysis

Frequently, brief dynamic psychotherapy is talked about as if it were something new, the latest fashion. It is not. Forerunners of brief psychotherapies are documented from earliest times in recorded human history, notably in Egypt and Greece. "Up to the beginning of the twentieth century methods of treatment were short-term" (Wolberg, 1980, p. 1)

As for brief dynamic psychotherapy, its history is as old as psychoanalysis itself. The two have evolved side by side. One could even argue that classical psychoanalysis has developed progressively from a form of brief therapy.

Freud's earliest cases were brief therapies, though he did not set out to plan his therapies to be short, whereas others did. Some of his contemporaries—Ferenczi and Rank foremost among them—set out to develop shortening techniques (Figure 1).

Then Franz Alexander and T. M. French (1946) started to experiment with modifications of the traditional technique: chair instead of the couch, varying frequency, deliberate interruptions prior to termination, etc. Their approach included the corrective emotional experience—the concept for which they are best known—as well as problem-solving.

The progress of brief therapies remained, however, strangely discontinuous. The question Gustafson asked ten

**Initially S. FREUD himself:**
**e.g. Bruno Walter was helped in 6 sessions in 1906**
**Gustav Mahler in 4 sessions in 1908**

**S. FERENCZI: "active therapy" (1920s)**
**O. RANK: "will therapy" (1930s)**
**W. STEKEL: "focused therapy" (1940s)**

**F. ALEXANDER & T. M. FRENCH:**
**"corrective emotional experience" (1940s)**

**P. SIFNEOS: "anxiety-provoking therapy" (1950s)**

**J. MANN: "time-limited psychotherapy" (1960s)**

**M. BALINT: "focal therapy" (1950s)**
**D. H. MALAN: scientific outcome research; TCP-link (1970s)**

**H. DAVANLOO: exhausting the pt.'s resistance**
**"trial therapy" (1980s)**

FIGURE 1.   Brief dynamic psychotherapy: its history
(main contributors; their key ideas; the most relevant decade)

years ago—"Why is it that the secret of brief psychotherapy keeps getting lost?" (Gustafson, 1981, p. 83)—remains unanswered. Time and again this complex secret has been rediscovered. Pioneers of brief analytic therapies periodically emerged and added their contribution to the arsenal of ideas and sophisticated shortening techniques: Sifneos, Mann, Balint, Malan, Davanloo, Horowitz, Gustafson, and others.

At the same time, psychoanalysis grew longer, and more weekly sessions were added. With "psycho-analysis the most easily identified tendency, . . . has been towards an *increase in the length of therapy*" (Malan, 1963, p. 6; italics as in original). This was stated thirty years ago; the situation does not seem to have changed much since then.

To sum up, resistance against shortening psychotherapy has been operating from the earliest days of psychoanalysis and all through its history. Today we could also add, at least in this country, that even training programmes grow longer year by year as training institutions for counsellors and psychotherapists increase their requirements in order to approximate their ideal of the prestigious training for long-term psychoanalysis . . .

## The self-sabotage
## of analytic psychotherapies

The tendency to resist shortening psychotherapy is there in each of us therapists. We can observe it operating in our colleagues and in ourselves. It is quite likely that the history of ever longer therapies "is repeated in a minor way by most of us who practice psychotherapy" (Gustafson, 1981, p. 83).

There are some apparently obvious and plausible reasons why analytically trained therapists should prefer the long-term to the short-term format. We have mentioned the great social pressure.

Another reason is that brief dynamic psychotherapy is very hard work. To do brief dynamic psychotherapy, the therapist has to overcome not only the patient's resistance, but also her own tendency to slip back to a more comfortable, more passive mode of doing therapy. Especially with highly resistant patients, it is all too easy to give in and stop confronting.

In private practice the rapid turnover of brief-therapy patients creates more administrative work and, above all, causes anxiety about insufficient referrals to replace those who have terminated therapy. Even if there is a long waiting list, some therapists might find it strenuous to face new patients rather than the more familiar ones who carry on in long-term therapy. Lengthening factors that might operate on the part of the therapist are listed in Figure 2.

On the whole, however, qualified psychotherapists are dedicated, hard-working, conscientious professionals who have the patient's interest at heart. If they were convinced that brief dynamic psychotherapy was the treatment of choice for a particular patient, they would not put their own comfort or financial or any other self-interest first.

Personal advantages do exist also for the therapist practising brief psychotherapy. In private practice, for instance, a patient in once-weekly brief psychotherapy would pay more per session than a patient in five-times-a-week long-term analysis. Moreover, in contrast to those in private practice, those who work in the public sector are under pressure to do short-term counselling and psychotherapy. Yet the latter, too, yearn to be able to do long-term work.

If we look back at what happened to practitioners of psychoanalysis since Freud and including Freud himself, and if we assume that their aim was to help patients in the most effective way, then we see a persistent self-defeating pattern or unconscious self-sabotage. It is a history of ever more ambitious aims, combined with the increasing use of less and less effective tools.

The aims of analysis have expanded to become very wide, to encompass the exploration of the earliest roots of the current disturbance, to explore the same problem from every angle, to "cure" the patient completely, to "cure" once and for all, to bring about a radical change of personality, and to uncover the entire realm of the patient's unconscious. In a way the ever deeper exploration of the unconscious became the paramount aim rather than achieving effective change in the patient.

The new techniques—the tools of classical psychoanalysis—adopted to achieve such overambitious aims were less rather than more effective than the previous ones had been. They were outright counterproductive. Most modern psychoanalysts, however, have long since corrected this

I
## PRINCIPAL FACTOR

(1) **Time.** Escape from linear time, i.e. from time's arrow. The lure of timelessness, i.e. of time's cycle, of the soothing experience of the "eternal return" in the rhythm of the sessions with no end in sight. The time factor is likely to be the motivating force behind most of the following factors.

II
## FACTORS INHERENT IN THE PSYCHOANALYTIC METHODOLOGY

(2) Rule of **free associations** (couch, relaxed atmosphere, sense of timelessness. See 1). (3) Therapist's **passivity** ("non-directive" neutrality, "blank screen"). (4) **Working through** the same problems from many angles and at various depths (assumptions: "the more the better", "the deeper the better", "the longer the better"). (5) Facilitating the development of **transference neurosis** and **regression** (once established, takes time to undo).

III
## FACTORS OPERATING IN PATIENTS

(6) **Resistance** of the unconscious against change, against being uncovered. (7) **Roots of neurosis** remote, in early childhood (takes time if we want to unravel it all. See 4). (8) **Overdetermination,** i.e. unconscious formations have more than one determinant (takes time if we want to unravel it all. See 4). (9) Patient's **dependence** and consequent passivity (related to 5). (10) Difficulties with **termination** (mainly related to 1, but also to 6 and 9).

FIGURE 2.

counterproductive trend. The rule of free association, together with the old-fashioned "blank-screen", passive therapist sitting behind the equally passive patient lying on the couch, allow the neurotic patient's constant attitude—mostly compliance or defiance—and negative transference to go on unchallenged for a very long time (chapter 3). The method by which the analyst gives accurate interpretations at the right time might still leave the patient's defence sys-

## IV
### FACTORS OPERATING IN MANY PSYCHOTHERAPISTS

(11) Therapeutic **perfectionism**. Setting far too ambitious aims for therapy (see 4, 8). The idea of curing completely and once and for all. (12) Increasing preoccupation or obsession with analysing ever **deeper** and **earlier** experiences (see 4, 5, 7, 8). (13) Scientific **curiosity** or **fascination** with the unconscious becomes stronger than the resolve to help the patient. (14) **Fear of confronting** the resistance (see 6) due to the fear of the patient's angry response and/or fear of hurting or losing the patient. (15) **Loss of self-confidence** or of faith in one's own ability to "cure" (see 11). (16) Resistance against brief, time-limited therapy because it is **strenuous** for the therapist. (17) **Social pressure** from colleagues against therapists practising brief, time-limited therapy.

## V
### FACTORS SPECIFIC TO PRIVATE PRACTICE

(18) Anxiety about **insufficient referrals** to replace brief-therapy patients who terminate. (19) High turnover of patients in brief therapy creates increased **administrative work**.

NOTE. The twelve lengthening factors listed by D.H. Malan (*A Study of Brief Psychotherapy*. New York: Plenum, 1963, pp. 8–9, 281) are incorporated in this list with modifications. Malan mentions the "sense of timelessness" (Stone, L. [1951]. Psychoanalysis and brief psychotherapy. *Psychoanal. Quart., 20*, 215 ), but without developing the idea further. He does not make a hypothesis about any possible principal lengthening factor that might underlie the others.

Lengthening factors in analytic psychotherapies since Freud

tem untouched and even strengthen the "defensive wall" behind which the true feelings hide. The idea that the patient will be helped mainly by promoting regression and transference neurosis in order to work through them is as dubious as is the concomitant increase in the number of sessions to five a week. Actually, transference neurosis might become a secondary problem in itself, which, in its turn, will take further time to resolve.

The first to sabotage his own work unwittingly was Freud himself. At the beginning he himself placed emphasis on a quick diagnosis and on the immediate resolution of the internal conflict. In the cases he reported as successes, he started with the symptom, kept the focus on the event in which the symptom occurred, and persistently inquired about it. In the cases of failure, he made it his main task to reconstruct, explain, and describe the repressed material. He neglected handling the resistance first or confronting the patient's characteristic attitude or bringing out the negative transference. He adopted the roundabout way of analysing the patient's dreams and was increasingly diverted by the details and complexity of the material produced through free associations.

### Time as the principal lengthening factor: a hypothesis

This process of self-sabotage can be reformulated by saying that analytic psychotherapists are eventually defeated by the patient's and their own unconscious. The unconscious by definition resists being uncovered and resists any change. What better way to ensure the permanence of the status quo than to lure the analyst into pursuing ever more ambitious aims whilst using increasingly less efficient tools?

The unconscious is blind to the requirements of reality. It is also timeless by its nature. "The wishes of the unconscious are timeless and promptly run counter to an offer of help in which time is limited" (Mann, 1973b, p. 10).

I believe that to the extent that analytic psychotherapies offer a space within which the timelessness of childhood—which coincides with the timelessness of the unconscious—can be re-experienced, they also awaken powerful resistances against its disruptions. In other words, analytic psychotherapies, by virtue of travelling in the realm of the

unconscious, carry an in-built resistance against shortening techniques.

Long-term, open-ended individual psychotherapy offers a
most soothing and seductive combination of both time's
arrow and time's cycle. Time's arrow or linear time is
used to establish the time structure, appointment times,
frequency and length of sessions, and holiday arrangements. These boundaries carve out a secure psychological
space from everyday reality. Time's cycle—that is, the soothing experience of eternal return—now appears within the
regular, predictable rhythm of recurrent sessions marked
out by time's arrow. Trust develops, we come into contact
with timelessness and oceanic feelings of eternal union.
Although there might be a "threat of disintegration and
dissolution" (Fubini, 1988, p. 315) of the self in this limitless
universe, we are protected against it by linear time boundaries, the end of the session. Long-term, open-ended psychotherapy creates a near-perfect balance between time's
arrow and time's cycle. However, this ideal arrangement is
shattered when the issue of termination comes up. Then the
confrontation with real time becomes dramatic. In time-
limited therapies, the struggle with the passage of time, with
real time, is present from the beginning.

Several authors have proposed a variety of explanations
and postulated a number of factors responsible for the trend
of ever longer therapies. The most comprehensive list is
probably the one Malan (1963, pp. 8–9, 281) has given us.
Nevertheless, none of the factors inherent in the psychoanalytic methodology, or operating on the part of the patient or
the therapist or in private practice—and not even all these
factors together—can account for the consistently powerful
and universal pull towards longer rather than shorter psychotherapies. To explain it, we need to pinpoint an equally
powerful and universal factor that affects us all.

I would like to put forward the hypothesis that this universal factor is time itself: our way of conceptualizing and
experiencing time, our fear of linear time—our fear of losses,
separations, endings, and ultimately our fear of death; our

need to escape from it into timelessness. The addiction to psychotherapy, pointed out by some analysts (Saul, 1972, p. 291), might simply be addiction to the experience of timelessness.

If we postulate time itself—our experience of it and our unconscious attitude to it—as the principal lengthening factor, two other irrational resistances fall into place as well. One is the resistance against intermittent or recurrent therapies, the other is resistance against group therapy.

We can understand the resistance against recurrent individual therapies if we think of them as repeated endings, as repeated disruptions that frustrate the tendency to become addicted to timelessness.

If it is true that there might be a trend among group analysts to give up groups progressively in order to do more individual work (Grotjahn, 1983, p. 258), as mentioned earlier, then the lure of timelessness might be fundamentally responsible for it. A group offers less chance to escape from reality and real time into timelessness than does the dyadic situation.

I have incorporated into Figure 2 Malan's 12 lengthening factors, with some modifications and additions. Most importantly, I added time itself as the principal lengthening factor that possibly underlies most, if not all, other factors included in the list. Malan does mention the "sense of timelessness" (Stone, 1951), but without considering it the central factor or developing the idea further. He does not make a hypothesis about any possible lengthening factor that might underlie the others.

## Rationale for shortening analytic psychotherapies

If the above hypothesis is accepted or appears at least plausible, then it is quite clear that it is the analytic therapist's professional duty to resist the unconscious temptation to allow the therapy to go on for too long. There are several other commonsensical reasons why analytic psychotherapies need shortening.

First, it is a question of overall effectiveness. The idea of "the longer the better" is very doubtful. For some patients, a brief therapy can yield better results than a long one. For many patients "the longer the better" might be true, provided we choose to disregard the law of diminishing returns. Cost-effectiveness of psychotherapy has to be considered not only in terms of money, but also in terms of the time and energy the patient puts into it. If the same result, or nearly the same result, can be obtained by investing half or even a tenth of his resources, is it not our ethical responsibility to offer the patient this more cost-, time-, and energy-effective alternative?

Second, cost-effectiveness becomes quite specifically the paramount issue if we look at the public sector. Because of lack of resources—not only in terms of time and money but also in terms of qualified personnel and adequate physical environment—long-term analytic psychotherapy is simply impracticable within public-sector health care. To practise it in a few cases would be grossly unfair vis-à-vis those remaining on the growing waiting lists. Indeed, economic expediency seems to be the only universally accepted argument in favour of brief psychotherapy. Unfortunately, the economic argument obscures the fact that planned, short-term, time-limited analytic therapy is not only cost-effective from the point of view of the care-giving services, but it is often the best form of treatment for the patient.

Those who hold brief psychotherapy in disdain tolerate it as a poor but often necessary substitute for the real thing. Those who are convinced of its effectiveness think differently. If we develop something out of need and using scarce resources, it does not mean that the result will be equally poor. Actually, the outcome might be better than where there is plenty. The Chinese developed their cuisine out of need, in the midst of famines, by learning to use the most unlikely ingredients with great ingenuity. Although short-term approaches tend to evolve in conditions of limited resources, their therapeutic value has to be assessed as opposed to being prejudged.

By now there is ample scientific evidence proving the effectiveness of brief analytic approaches, including time-limited group analysis. Alexander and French (1946), Butcher and Koss (1978), Grand, Rechetnick, Podrug, and Schwager (1985), Høglend, Sørlie, Sørbye, Heyerdahl, and Amlo (1992), Husby (1985), McCallum and Piper (1990), Marziali (1984; Marziali & Sullivan, 1980), Noel et al. (1985), Piper (1992; Piper et al., 1985, 1986, 1990, 1991), Sifneos (1981), Strupp (1980), and Yung (1978) are among the many who have conducted research in this field. Perhaps the most systematic research was done by Malan (1963, 1976a, 1976b, 1980a; Malan & Osimo, 1992).

All evidence indicates that planned short-term analytic therapies are more than just a poor, barely tolerable substitute for the much-sought-after real thing, namely long, open-ended psychoanalysis. Regardless of the availability or lack of resources, planned short-term dynamic psychotherapy is the treatment of choice for a considerable proportion of patients.

Third, there are also subjective reasons why one would prefer to practise brief rather than long-term psychotherapy. For instance, one's personality might be more suited to it. There is scope, however, for both: for those psychotherapists who prefer long-term as well as for those who prefer short-term work.

Finally, it is possible to think of many wrong reasons why a patient or a therapist might prefer short-term therapy. The most frequent wrong reason among patients is that of not wanting to go "too deep"; in other words, they simply have poor motivation for change. On the part of the therapist, there might be unconscious reasons, such as magical fantasies of curing someone instantly, omnipotence, rivalry with "slow" colleagues, and so on. None of these and other possible wrong reasons is specific to brief psychotherapy. Obviously, any therapist who is keen on brief work because of such hidden, self-orientated destructive motives is either in need of psychotherapeutic help herself or should not be a psychotherapist at all.

No-one claims that short-term therapy is suitable for every patient or that it should replace all forms of long-term treatment. As a general rule, the earlier the psychic damage, the more likely it is that the patient might need longer rather than shorter therapy. Moreover, long-term psychoanalysis is a unique learning experience, and certainly invaluable for anyone who wishes to become a psychotherapist. Nevertheless, the most effective way of doing psychoanalytic therapy is also the shortest one. If properly conducted, even the briefest form of therapy, namely the focused, single-session therapy, has positive consequences (Bloom, 1981, p. 180; Budman, 1981a, pp. 2–3; Davanloo, 1978e; Hoyt, Rosenbaum, & Talmon, 1992). In any case, psychotherapy should be as short as possible and only as long as the patient really needs it.

We can overcome the resistance against shortening techniques if we as therapists pay more attention to time itself, to our experience of it, to how our work is affected by it. Whatever we do, we should heed the warning against over-treating the patient (Foulkes, 1975, p. 73).

*CHAPTER TWO*

# Brief dynamic psychotherapy

## *What makes a therapy psychoanalytic?*

This chapter is about brief psychoanalytic or psycho-dynamic therapy. Before discussing what brief or short-term mean, we have to clarify the nature of the process that we are going to shorten.

---

This chapter is based on four talks, two of which I have given within the framework of a one-day seminar organized for a mixed audience of nurses, psychologists, psychiatrists, counsellors, and other health workers at St. James Hospital, Portsmouth, in March 1993. I also delivered two lectures in Hungarian on the same topic, one in Targu Mures, Transylvania, Romania, in March 1994, and the other at the XI National Scientific Conference of the Hungarian Psychological Society, held in Debrecen, Hungary, in April 1994. The talks attempted to condense my thoughts about brief dynamic psychotherapy, which I have explored in many lectures here and abroad since 1983—the year the idea of the four triangles (Figure 7, this chapter) came to me.

The following is an attempt to give the briefest possible formulation of what, in my view, constitutes the essence of analytic psychotherapy:

*In order to do psychoanalytic psychotherapy, one has to create a special space in which the past can reappear in the here-and-now, a space in which past emotional conflicts are re-lived and understood with clarity, and in which new solutions to old problems are found.*

The special space is created by the boundaries. The idea of working in the transference is also embedded in this formulation. The question of what makes a therapy psychoanalytic can be answered with two key concepts: *boundaries* and *transference*.

## Boundaries and therapeutic space

The special space that is the therapeutic situation is established and maintained by the therapist through the boundaries. Boundaries may be seen to have three functions. One is to carve out a special space from everyday life. The other two are to create a secure base for the therapeutic process and to set a baseline for observation.

The issue of boundaries is often neglected. Such neglect is mainly due to a certain confusion between the frame in which the therapy takes place and the process itself, confusion between the therapist's role as administrator and manager of the therapeutic situation and her role in the process. Moreover, some therapists have a misguided fear of being too "directive" if they set the boundaries clearly and firmly.

The importance of handling the therapeutic boundaries properly cannot be overemphasized. This is especially true in a hospital setting, where the medical model prevails and there is no general understanding of what psychotherapeutic boundaries mean and why they are necessary at all. Of course, medical practice has its own boundaries, but they are completely different.

Boundaries are necessary in order to do any psycho-therapy. No psychotherapy can take place without boundaries. However, some boundaries are uniquely psy-choanalytic.

We can roughly group the boundaries in four categories: the boundaries of *place, time, conduct required,* and *relationship* (Figure 3). This sequence moves from the simpler to the more complex.

Here are a few examples of what is meant by boundaries:

EXAMPLE 1: *boundary of place*

We are in *another room* today. The patient becomes uncooperative, finds it difficult to talk. When he was a child, the patient's needs were not heard, not registered by busy and restless parents. They also moved house several times, so that he kept on losing the friends he made, playmates, schoolmates. He felt powerless. He especially hated his father for that. Now he feels powerless with his boss and with the therapist.

---

**PLACE**
**kept constant, comfortable, simple, friendly, etc.**

**TIME**
**kept regular, fixed, convenient, etc.**

**CONDUCT REQUIRED**
**regularity, punctuality, suspended action**

**RELATIONSHIP(S)**
**therapist's attitude, confidentiality, consistency, reliability, honesty yet no self-disclosure, abstinence**

---

FIGURE 3. Boundaries: categories.

EXAMPLE 2: *boundary of place*

*Noises* from the other room. Sudden fear of other people invading. The patient dreads that they have heard what he has disclosed so far. In adolescence father would always interfere when the patient had a cosy get-together with mother. He was jealous and wanted his wife's whole attention for himself all the time.

Both examples concern the boundary of place. In the first example, the therapist could not or has failed to ensure that the same room would be available for the duration of therapy. In the second she was unable or failed to ensure that it would be sound-proof. These examples also show how boundary violations constitute useful material for therapeutic work. Such violations cannot be avoided, even by the therapist at times, but as long as they are accurately observed and taken up, they become yet more grist to the mill.

The following are examples concerning the boundary of time:

EXAMPLE 3: *boundary of time*

A female patient is a *chronic late-comer*. She is typically passive-resistant and compliant. She had a controlling, sharp-tongued, intrusive mother. The patient is angry about the therapeutic situation and fearful of not having control. Moreover, she is afraid of overburdening the therapist. She herself becomes very anxious when someone close to her is late.

EXAMPLE 4: *boundary of time*

The same patient *misses* the first session after the Christmas holidays. Separation anxiety.

In both examples it is the patient who attacks the boundaries of time. If the therapist lets such events pass and ignores them, then she is colluding with the patient's

neurosis. The psychoanalytic therapist's task in such instances is to make the patient focus on his (in this case, her)
pattern of behaviour, help him to discover his emotions in
the here-and-now vis-à-vis the therapist and the therapeutic
situation and connect those emotions with the past.

Let us see an example concerning the conduct required
of a patient who is in psychoanalytic therapy.

EXAMPLE 5: *boundary of conduct required*

Three minutes before the end of the session this 35-
year-old patient, a mother of two young children, gets
up from her chair and *sits on the floor* at the therapist's
feet. The therapist says nothing. The patient is aware of
having done something against the rules. She feels
uncomfortable, anxious, laughs, and makes jokey
comments on her own action. Exactly on time, the
therapist gets up and gently but firmly says: "We have
to finish now."

This was a violation on the part of the patient of the rule
of *suspended action*. The patient acted out her wish to be
taken care of by the therapist, as if she were a small child.
The therapist reacted correctly. She neither colluded with
the patient nor retaliated. With her gentle manner (i.e. non-
verbal communication), she also showed understanding of
the young mother's problem. As it encapsulated much of the
patient's internal and interpersonal difficulties, this inci-
dent became the focal reference point in the subsequent
phases of therapy.

The conduct required from both patient and therapist is
to respect the boundaries of place and time. In addition in a
psychoanalytic therapy there should be suspended action.
Obviously no psychotherapist can or should force the
patient to do anything. However, a psychoanalytic therapist
will not let the patient get away with ignoring or transgress-
ing the boundaries without bringing the matter to the
patient's full awareness. The therapist will always try to
understand the attack on the boundaries in terms of the
patient's characteristic pattern of relating. She will help the

patient to discover the links with analogous problems in relationships he has now and had in the past.

While no psychotherapy can exist without boundaries, different types of therapy have different boundaries. The boundary of suspended action is specific to the psychoanalytic approach. The idea is that both the patient and the therapist refrain from any action except talking. The patient is encouraged to express his feelings and emotions as fully as possible instead of acting upon them. Refraining from action increases the internal pressure, which, in its turn, helps to put the experience into words. The therapist accepts unconditionally the feelings the patient experiences and verbalizes, including the hostile feelings towards herself. Moreover, the therapist monitors her own feelings, but without talking about them.

This leads us to the boundaries of the *therapeutic relationship,* which are the therapist's attitude, abstinence, confidentiality, consistency, reliability, and honesty but without self-disclosure. Among these boundaries the last one is more typical of psychoanalytic therapies than of other forms of psychotherapy.

EXAMPLE 6: *boundary of relationship* (no self-disclosure)

"From where do you come?" Some patients believe I come from Greece because of my name, some assume that I am Austrian, German, or Czech because of my accent. A few guess correctly that I come from Hungary. In each case I say the same—namely, that I don't answer personal questions—and explain why. If I did, the patient's freedom to express himself would be restricted.

EXAMPLE 7: *boundary of relationship* (no self-disclosure):

"Where are you going on holiday? Somewhere nice?" The answer is the same as above.

All these questions patients ask are geared to change the therapeutic relationship into a social one. They seek a non-analytic, non-therapeutic kind of closeness. Often they aim at gaining more control. The therapist has to resist these attempts.

The other boundaries of the therapeutic relationship—the therapist's attitude, abstinence, confidentiality, consistency, reliability, honesty—are characteristic of non-analytic therapies as well. At the end of this chapter we will return to the first of these—the therapist's attitude, which is of fundamental importance.

Finally, it has to be mentioned that I have taken the term from the language of group analysis. I find "boundary" clearer and more precise than most of the other equivalents used in the literature such as arrangements, conditions, contract, devices, frame, framework, ground rules, obligations, parameters, requirements, routines, setting, structure, therapeutic management, etc. (Figure 4).

---

**arrangements**

**conditions**

**contract**

**devices**

**frame, framework**

**ground rules**

**obligations**

**parameters**

**requirements**

**routines**

**setting**

**structure**

**therapeutic management**

---

FIGURE 4.   Boundaries:
alternative terms and expressions found in the literature.

---

**via the BOUNDARIES
the therapist creates a**

**special, safe space**

**psychological space**

**secure base (Bowlby)**

**container (Bion)**

*vas hermeticum* **(Jung)**

**facilitating, holding environment (Winnicott)**

**group matrix (Foulkes)**

**alternative system (Garland)**

**i. e.
THE THERAPEUTIC SITUATION**

---

FIGURE 5.   The therapeutic situation:
terms and expressions describing it.

To conclude this section on boundaries, it has to be reiterated that all these boundaries—place, time, conduct required, relationship (Figure 3)—together define the special, safe psychological space in which the therapy takes place. This space can be called the therapeutic situation; it can also be described in many other ways. Different authors use a variety of terms to characterize it: secure base (Bowlby), container (Bion), *vas hermeticum* (Jung), holding, facilitating environment (Winnicott), group matrix (Foulkes), alternative system (systems theory). (See Figure 5.)

## Transference

Now let us turn to the other key ingredient that makes a therapy psychoanalytic: the transference. With the help of the boundaries, we have created a special space, we have carved out the therapeutic situation from everyday life. What happens in it? The answer is in the definition given at the start:

*In order to do psychoanalytic psychotherapy, one has to create a special space in which the past can reappear in the here-and-now, a space in which past emotional conflicts are re-lived and understood with clarity, and in which new solutions to old problems are found.*

The most important thing that happens in the therapeutic situation is that we "work in the transference". This phrase, however, with the preposition "in", suggests to me that we are sitting in midst of the transference with no reference to reality. Therefore, I prefer to say that we work "through" the transference.

First, here is a definition of the term "transference" as I understand and use it:

*Transference is the phenomenon by which patterns of behaviour, responses, the underlying feelings and concomitant anxieties, which have been developed in early childhood, reappear in later relationships, in particular in relation to the therapist and the boundaries of the therapeutic situation itself.*

Usually these patterns are the child's healthy and reasonable response to some unhealthy and unreasonable situation, mostly in his relationship with his parents. As the child grows, he remains programmed, so to speak, to respond with the old patterns in any close relationship. In other words, the old patterns become inappropriate, maladaptive.

For the symbols appearing in the following examples, please refer to The Four Triangles (Figure 7, on p. 37). I devised this graphic representation of the process of analytic psychotherapy for teaching purposes in 1983. The symbols are explained in more detail further on.

EXAMPLE 8: *pattern in childhood* (P)

Tim's parents had a very unhappy marriage. His mother used to pack her suitcases, drag along her four children, and leave the house, only to return after a few days. She devoted her energies to the sickly youngest baby. The hard-working husband was never at home. Tim, the eldest, was neglected. At age 5 he negotiated his way on his own to attend his first day at school. Three years later, after his father's premature death, he was sent to boarding school. There he was bullied by the other boys and suffered daily ritual humiliations and severe beatings. His pleas to mother remained unanswered. There was no escape. Tim's healthy response to this unbearable situation was to develop a powerfully tough survival strategy.

One: Maintaining of co-operative, compliant, passive, self-effacing behaviour towards others (D = defence). He had no choice.

Two: Cutting off, repressing, denying (D) all his feelings of hurt, pain, rage, sadness ($-X$ = negative feelings).

Three: Becoming highly independent, autonomous, not needing anyone (D = [character] defences).

In later life he became a very successful manager in an international corporation and hopeless in close relationships. We can now look at the problem as Tim presented it to the therapist—the so-called presenting problem.

EXAMPLE 9: *the presenting problem* (C)

The same patient (Tim) feels low, depressed, unworthy of love, and he wants to leave his girlfriend, Jill. He cannot talk to her, does not feel anything for her, cannot tolerate (D) her touching him or telling him "I love you". He is anxious (A = anxiety) and feels like running away. He has no idea of what is happening to him, what is underneath it all (X = true feelings, unknown).

We can analyse Tim's presenting problem with the aid of the triangle of conflict in Figure 6. The pattern Tim devel-

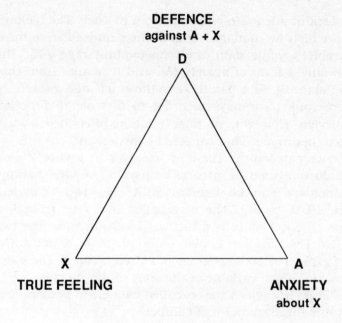

FIGURE 6.    The triangle of conflict.

oped—had to develop—in childhood is a powerful defensive fortress (D) that by now has become a trap for life. The main building blocks of his defensive system are: defensive compliance, passivity in behaviour; isolation, repression and denial of feelings; distancing himself from any closeness. Any attempt by others to get close to him raises his anxiety (A). He does not know what he feels (X). Actually, he "confesses" that he is unable to feel anything. That conviction makes him feel guilty towards Jill and unworthy of her love or anyone's love, and it undermines his self-image.

The reader might think that he does know after all what he feels: he feels guilty . . . Yes, but the X—his true feeling, unknown even to himself at this stage—about which he is anxious (A), against which he defends himself (D), is another feeling. Let us remind ourselves what happened to him in childhood: neglect, constant threats of abandonment, father's premature death, abuse at school over several years, lack of adequate response from mother. The feelings against which he managed to immunize himself were hurt, unbearable psychic pain, and concomitant rage (–X). The guilt is only a form of anxiety (A), and it results from that rage (chapter 3). Tim had to keep these feelings away from his conscious awareness in order to be able to function and survive. However, in close relationships they always threaten to surface. That causes the anxiety (A).

Now we can look at the four triangles in Figure 7 as a visual aid to study the process of psychoanalytic therapy. Some readers will be familiar with the "two triangles" (Malan, 1979, p. 80). The diagram of the "four triangles" (Molnos, 1984, 1986b) is a further development of the two triangles. The notation is also different. Most importantly, the patient's true feelings are symbolized by an X, the independent unknown variable at the start of the therapy.

The large triangle is the so-called triangle of person, and it contains three triangles of conflict.

So far we have talked about the triangle of conflict to illustrate Tim's presenting problem in the relationship with his girlfriend. This is a current relationship indicated by a C (= current). We have also sketched his original (P) internal conflict with his parents, especially his mother. P indicates significant relationships in the remote past, mostly with the parents (P = past, parents; coincidentally and luckily for us, both words begin with the same letter).

Finally, T stands for what happens in the here-and-now, in the therapeutic situation, and in relation to the therapist. We also say that T stands for transference. Again by lucky coincidence the relevant terms—transference, therapist, therapeutic situation—start with a T . . .

The usual sequence is as follows. The patient comes with his problem. No matter how he presents it, while we explore it, we soon find out that the core of the problem is some disturbance in his relationships with others. As we take his history, we look for patterns, and we discover similar patterns in his past. Finally, sooner or later we see the same pattern appearing in the here-and-now. Knowingly or not,

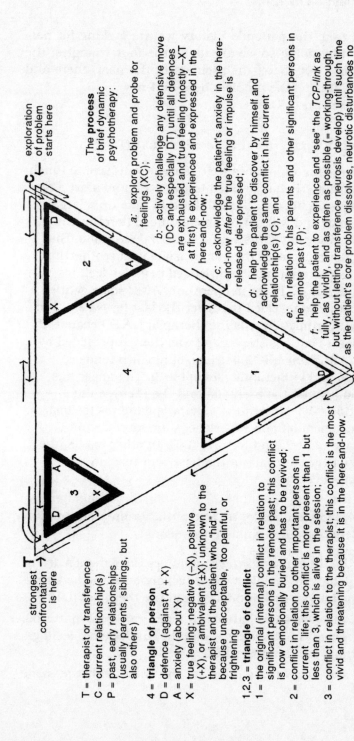

exploration of problem starts here

strongest confrontation is here

**The process** of brief dynamic psychotherapy:

*a:* explore problem and probe for feelings (XC);

*b:* actively challenge any defensive move (DC and especially DT) until all defences are exhausted and true feeling (mostly −XT at first) is experienced and expressed in the here-and-now;

*c:* acknowledge the patient's anxiety in the here-and-now *after* the true feeling or impulse is released, de-repressed;

*d:* help the patient to discover by himself and acknowledge the same conflict in his current relationship(s) (C); and

*e:* in relation to his parents and other significant persons in the remote past (P);

*f:* help the patient to experience and "see" the *TCP-link* as fully, as vividly, and as often as possible (= working-through, but without letting transference neurosis develop) until such time as the patient's core problem dissolves, neurotic disturbances no longer recur, and therapy can be terminated.

Copyright © 1983 by Angela Molnos.

T = therapist or transference
C = current relationship(s)
P = past, early relationships (usually parents, siblings, but also others)

**4 = triangle of person**
D = defence (against A + X)
A = anxiety (about X)
X = true feeling: negative (−X), positive (+X), or ambivalent (±X); unknown to the therapist and the patient who "hid" it because unacceptable, too painful, or frightening

**1,2,3 = triangle of conflict**
1 = the original (internal) conflict in relation to significant persons in the remote past; this conflict is now emotionally buried and has to be revived;
2 = conflict in relation to other important persons in current life; this conflict is more present than 1 but less than 3, which is alive in the session;
3 = conflict in relation to the therapist; this conflict is the most vivid and threatening because it is in the here-and-now.

*Note.* There is a coloured variant of this diagram in which the surfaces of the triangles are: pale yellow (1), orange (2), flame red (3), blue (4).

FIGURE 7. The Four Triangles

Literature (relevant to the diagram): Malan, 1979, p. 80; Davanloo, 1980, p. 52; Molnos, 1984, p. 120.

when we take the patient's history we are looking for patterns, and by doing so we are using the four triangles: the conflict now, out there; the problem in the past, there and then; and, finally, the problem here-and-now.

Let us return to Tim.

EXAMPLE 10: *pattern in the here-and-now* (T)

One day Tim announces that soon he will have to finish his therapy. He has decided to leave Jill and start a new business on his own. He will need to take up a large bank loan and will not be able to afford therapy any longer. Knowing of his sound financial situation, the therapist recognizes the money issue as a red herring. She realizes that unacknowledged negative feelings towards her (–XT) are in operation. After some gentle pressure it is revealed that over the last few weeks Tim has felt warmly towards the therapist (+XT) because of her help. That positive feeling was then superseded by fear (A) and anger (–X) because of his own tender feelings and vulnerability (chapter 3). The anger has turned against the therapist and the therapeutic situation (–XT). Instead of acknowledging his feelings, he cuts them off and experiences the impulse to distance himself and to leave (DT). In other words, the same pattern appears in the here-and-now, in the transference.

Finally, to sum up, let us attempt a formulation of what working through the transference means:

1. that the therapist *observes*, monitors the patient's defensive pattern of behaviour and responses in the *here-and-now* vis-à-vis the boundaries and the therapist (DT);

2. that she helps the patient to focus on these patterns, *experience* and *express* fully the underlying feelings, emotions and impulses (XT);

3. that she helps the patient to *link* them with the same

emotions and patterns of defensive behaviour in his *past* and *current* relationships (DAX/TCP);

4.  that she helps the patient to *change* those maladaptive patterns of behaviour and responses in the here-and-now as well as out there (D/TC).

## What makes a dynamic (or psychoanalytic) psychotherapy brief (or short-term)?

We have outlined the essentials of what makes a therapy psychoanalytic—namely, the boundaries that create the therapeutic space and the transference work that is the main process within that space. Now we can focus on three major ingredients that make a dynamic or psychoanalytic therapy brief. One is the early confrontation of the resistance by which we shorten the therapy at the beginning. The other two ingredients are the high activity on the therapist's part and the therapist's overall attitude in brief therapy.

First, we start by clarifying some of the terminology and by drawing a general comparison between the characteristics of long and brief dynamic psychotherapies.

### Terminology

From here on, the name I am using is "brief dynamic psychotherapy" (or its abbreviation, BDP). Also, the terms "dynamic" and "analytic" are used interchangeably, not quite in their exact meaning.

"Dynamic" is shorthand for "psychodynamic", which means that it is based on the conceptual frame of reference established by Freud. In other words, "dynamic", or "psychodynamic", or "analytic", or "psychoanalytic" means that psychic phenomena are the result of a combination of different forces (partly unconscious emotional drives and peremptory urges, and partly unconscious intentions). They exert pressure on each other, creating intrapsychic or internal conflict. Such conflicts occur within relationships all our lives. These concepts imply the existence of the unconscious, and therefore:

1. the production of derivatives of repressed material;
2. compromise formations;
3. resistance of the unconscious to being uncovered;
4. defence mechanisms against painful or unacceptable feelings, such as repression, projection, introjection, transference and so on (see Figure 10, in chapter 3);
5. the structural division of the psyche into ego, id, and superego.

"Dynamic psychotherapy" stands in contrast to behavioural, cognitive, and other forms of psychotherapies that are not designed to uncover the unconscious mechanisms but attempt to deal with the patient's problems on other levels.

Although combinations of dynamic, analytic, didactic, behavioural, cognitive, emotive, suggestive, hypnotic, and other elements appear to varying degrees in most psychotherapies, it is customary to choose a term to indicate the main ingredient and, with it, the professional identity of the therapist.

Strictly speaking, "dynamic" and "psychoanalytic" are not the same. "Dynamic" is the broader, more comprehensive, and more flexible concept, while "psychoanalytic" is the more specific. It can be argued that a therapy should be called "psychoanalytic" only if it adheres to the techniques and devices used in classical psychoanalysis, including the rule of free association, facilitating the development of regression and transference neurosis and the use of the couch. These features are eliminated from brief therapies, which, according to this view, can only be called "dynamic", but not "analytic" or "psychoanalytic". For our purposes, however, it is important to retain the free use of these terms to remind ourselves of the psychoanalytic roots and nature of the brief dynamic psychotherapy as distinct from other non-analytic brief therapies (e.g. behavioural, cognitive).

Students of psychotherapy often wonder about the difference between "brief", "short-term", and "time-limited". "*Brief*" and "*short-term*" are interchangeable overall terms. "Brief dynamic psychotherapy" is more used in Britain, "short-term dynamic psychotherapy" more in America. They indicate any psychoanalytically based psychotherapy with a limited number of sessions. The question of how brief is brief, how short is short, can be answered by saying that the meaning of these terms is a convention. Generally, it is accepted that a therapy can be called brief (or short) if it consists of anything from 1 to 30, or even 40 sessions, usually once weekly, over a period of one year or less.

The expression "*time-limited*" is used for a brief dynamic psychotherapy with the total number of sessions fixed in advance and a fixed termination date agreed beforehand (e.g. Mann) or with this plan being subject to review (e.g. Malan). Other brief dynamic psychotherapies are open-ended (e.g. Davanloo).

Another frequently heard expression is "*focal therapy*". It refers to a technical aspect of brief psychotherapies—namely, that we focus on selected problem areas that cause difficulties for the patient. The characteristic "focal" stands in contrast to psychoanalysis, where free association is the method and the tendency is to explore the whole realm of a patient's unconscious. The term "focal therapy" is mainly connected with the names of Michael Balint and David Malan, but it is now used by many others as well.

## Comparison of "long" and "brief" dynamic psychotherapy

The features that differ in psychoanalysis and in brief dynamic psychotherapy are listed in Figure 8. For those readers who are well-versed in the theory and practice of

[5 to 15 years] **ONE YEAR or less**

[3 to 5 times a week] **ONCE WEEKLY**

[couch] **FACE TO FACE**

Sense of [timelessness] **SPEED & progress**

Therapist is [less active] **more ACTIVE**

Pt.'s [free associations] **attention is FOCUSED**

Focus on the [past] **present, out there (C)**
**& HERE-AND-NOW (T)**

T. [interprets] **CHALLENGES resistance (T/DAX)**

[Transference neurosis] **T/D IMMEDIATELY**

[Regression] **Strengthening the pt.'s EGO**

Focus on [exploring the unconscious]
**the problem-PATTERN**

Focus on [sexual impulses]
**LOSS, ABANDONMENT, RAGE (–X)**
**& problem-solving**

FIGURE 8.   Brief dynamic psychotherapy:
its characteristics compared with
the lengthening characteristics of traditional psychoanalysis
(the latter are in brackets and crossed out)

long-term psychoanalysis, the list is very easy to understand. For those who are not familiar with psychoanalysis, some explanation might be needed.

When one reads a textbook on BDP, the implicit comparison is always with psychoanalysis. The very terms "brief" or "short-term" therapy have been coined precisely in contrast to classical psychoanalysis. This might be somewhat confusing for those readers who follow brief, non-analytic approaches, such as cognitive and behavioural therapies, and whose basis of comparison, therefore, is a different one.

So, let us return to this comparison. If we want to do brief dynamic psychotherapy, we have to look again at both the boundaries and the way we work through the transference. We will have to readjust the time boundaries. We said that a therapy of 40 sessions or fewer can be called brief. This statement has to be qualified because a therapy of fewer than 40 sessions can be a failed therapy, in which case we cannot call it brief. A therapy that is terminated prematurely—for instance, because the patient drops out—is not a brief therapy. The therapy has to be brief by design, not by default.

For a therapy to be called "brief", in other words, it has to be planned to be such. The therapist has to set out deliberately to create the conditions for it and find ways to accelerate the process. Setting the time boundaries in advance is not enough in itself. Moreover, it has to be noted that although most brief therapists do establish preset time-limits, not all do so (e.g. Davanloo).

First of all the therapist has to be confident that good, productive work can be done within the given time limits. Confidence, optimism, realism, and a sense of speed have to permeate the encounter. The brief dynamic therapist tends to be more active and to intervene more often than an analyst. The time pressure and the patient's anxiety are used to motivate the patient to work intensively together with the therapist. Both make sure that each hour counts. Both experience that what makes a difference is not the absolute length of time, but what we do with it.

Even the physical environment—what I call the boundary of place—is consonant with this liveliness of a brief dynamic psychotherapy session, of working hard together. There is no couch, and the sessions are conducted face to face. While the classical psychoanalyst may try to create a working environment that induces the patient to sink into a softly lit, cosy dream-zone in which timelessness prevails, the therapist who practises brief dynamic psychotherapy prefers to work with the patient in a room devoid of symbolic references to the dim depths of the psyche. Accordingly, her room is well-lit, and it is and furnished and decorated in a friendly, simple fashion.

Instead of the patient's attention becoming unfocused and meandering from one idea to the next (i.e instead of free-associating), both the patient and the therapist focus their attention on selected problem areas. The aim is to clarify and explore these problem areas and to deal with them. Since Freud's times, when the emphasis was on the repression of sexual impulses at the roots of neuroses, there has been a shift towards issues of loss, abandonment, threat of abandonment, and concomitant repressed rage as the most frequently found background to psychic disturbances nowadays. This change is reflected in all psychotherapies, including BDP.

The focus is on the patient's current problems. The past will be explored not for its own sake, but only inasmuch as it interferes with or constitutes an obstacle in the here-and-now and out there in the patient's current life. All this amounts to one single major difference: contrary to what happens in classical psychoanalysis, in brief dynamic psychotherapy regression and transference neurosis are discouraged by working through the transference responses as soon as they appear and thus strengthening the adult ego.

Transference neurosis is defined as "an artificial neurosis into which the manifestations of the transference tend to become organized. It is built around the relationship with the analyst" (Laplanche & Pontalis, 1973, p. 462). It is not allowed to develop or consolidate in brief dynamic psychotherapy, where each transference reaction is confronted and worked through as soon as it appears.

"Ego strength" is a much used and useful term, but not easy to define. According to Wolberg (1977, p. 4), ". . . it connotes the positive personality assets that will enable the individual to overcome his anxieties, to yield secondary gains of his illness, and to acquire new, more adequate defenses." We could also say that ego strength is the patient's capacity to hold on to his own identity despite psychic pain, distress, turmoil, and conflict between opposing internal forces as well as the demands of reality (see also Brown & Pedder, 1979, p. 184). The development of transference neurosis reduces the ego strength and, conversely, each successful challenge of a transference reaction increases it.

## The importance of the beginning

The question about any "brief" therapy is whether we shorten the time at the beginning or at the end. In the latter case we have premature termination—unfinished, incomplete therapy. Only if we shorten the time at the beginning can we talk about brief therapy in any proper sense of the word. We achieve this by going to the heart of the trouble very fast. The essential shortening technique consists in using the first hour, the first minutes, of the therapeutic encounter to maximum effect. It means recognizing the problem-pattern very early on, reaching out to the patient's true self beyond the resistance as fast as the patient can bear that degree of closeness. How fast the patient can give up his self-crippling defensive fortress will depend more on his ego-strength than on his pathology. Davanloo (1980e) uses the first encounter as a so-called "trial therapy" to find out whether the patient has sufficient ego-strength to stand up to his kind of confrontation of the resistance. If the patient's thought processes become confused, he backs off and reverts to a more conventional method. Once the defensive wall is out of the way, we can spend the rest of our precious time on working on the problem via the transference.

So the beginning phase of brief dynamic psychotherapy is very short. As in any good dynamic psychotherapy, so in brief dynamic psychotherapy, too, the middle phase is the working through. The resistance might return, but in a milder form. If and when it does, it is dealt with immediately. In the end phase we have to make sure that feelings around separation are resolved. However, the therapist must be alert to the issue of loss and separation at all times. They are the prominent theme in brief dynamic psychotherapy. Both patient and therapist are aware that they will be together only for a short spell of time. That touches on many old feelings and important memories, which can and must be worked through.

Let us have another look at the four triangles in Figure 7 and at the example of how Tim starts therapy. Like all patients, he comes with a problem (C), which he presents as he perceives it.

EXAMPLE 9 (repeated): *the presenting problem* (C)

Tim feels low, depressed, unworthy of love, and he wants to leave his girlfriend Jill. He cannot talk to her, does not feel anything for her, cannot tolerate (D) her touching him or telling him "I love you". He is anxious (A = anxiety) and feels like running away. He has no idea what is happening to him, what is underneath it all (X = true feelings, unknown).

He is sincere, but unwittingly he skates over the painful, disturbing bits. What he resists facing is his repressed murderous rage directed at Jill and, of course, at his mother. At this very early point the therapist has *two choices*.

Choice number one: The therapist can carry on listening with empathy. By doing so, she signals her total acceptance of whatever the patient has to say. The therapist's interventions are designed to follow the patient and encourage him to carry on expressing himself. That is the *beginning of a long therapy*.

Choice number two: The therapist listens also with empathy and very carefully to what the patient says and does not say, and pays special attention to the non-verbal signals as well. She knows that every patient comes with a mixture of motivation and resistance. She wants to identify quickly the true feelings beyond the resistance. She sets out to help the patient discover and recognize his own resistance, his own self-defeating mechanism as fast as the patient can bear to do so. That is the *beginning of a brief therapy.*

Tim says he feels bad—a bad person. "No one should have to put up with me. I do not feel anything for anyone. Jill has been very good to me, supported me a lot. I just want to run away." At this point the brief therapist decides to focus on the statement, "Jill has been very good to me." Generalities follow. She asks for a concrete example when Jill did something good. She asks for the nitty-gritty of the interaction between the two of them. Where were they? Who did, said what? Word by word, blow by blow. At what point did he have the impulse to escape? What did he really feel, experience, then?

The more the therapist presses for the true feeling in the current situation (XC), the more the anxiety in the here-and-now intensifies (AT). Tim starts using evasive manoeuvres. "I feel confused." . . . "What was your question?" . . . "I don't remember." He averts his gaze. The therapist challenges him again and again about his feelings with her, until he becomes fully aware of his internal conflict in the here-and-now (DAX/T) and links it with similar conflicts in the past (DAX/P). Then they can go back to C—that is, the current internal conflict (DAX/C)—on a deeper, less defensive level.

## Transference needs no time

To sum up:

1. The only way of doing effective psychoanalytic therapy is working through the transference.

2. The most effective shortening technique is to shorten the beginning of the therapy. Therefore, if we want the therapy to be effective and short, we have to start recognizing the transference in the first session—preferably during the first minutes of the first session.

Generally it is assumed that the transference builds up slowly in the course of many sessions. This assumption simply does not tally with daily clinical observation. Actually, the transference is there from the outset, even before the patient arrives! We don't need to wait until it builds up. All we need to do is to recognize it promptly.

There are many *signals*, including the therapist's countertransference feelings, indicating that the patient's transference has been mobilized and is in operation. Here are a few:

• the patient's response to the therapist, to the here-and-now, is blatantly at variance with the real situation;

• the patient talks about other people, but actually what he says can be easily applied to the therapist or how he perceives her and the therapeutic situation;

• the patient smiles out of context;

• the patient's non-verbal communications indicate irritation, anger, etc. in contrast to his compliant verbal communications;

• the therapist feels stuck;

• time does not seem to pass, is slowed down;

• the atmosphere is heavy, the therapist gets drowsy.

The following examples show the diagnostic value of the first moments, as well as the fact that we do not have to cultivate the transference. It is there already, waiting for the therapist to fit into it, even before the encounter takes place.

### EXAMPLE 11: *transference needs no time*

A patient arrives for the first session. The therapist opens the door, and he asks loudly before stepping through: *"What shall I call you? Mrs, Miss, Doctor, Anne?"* This is a very anxious and highly defended patient who is unable to relate.

### EXAMPLE 12: *transference needs no time*

Another patient arrives 20 minutes late to the first session. She is very angry with the therapist. When the latter asks her about it, the patient replies: *"I did not understand the directions you gave me on the phone. . . . You have a foreign accent. . . No, I did not ask you to repeat. I would not have understood you the second time either. . ."* The patient spent the best part of her life raging against her ambitious mother, who came to this country from Poland, never lost her native accent, and never ceased pushing her only daughter towards high performance and success . . .

### EXAMPLE 13: *transference needs no time*

Coming 20 minutes late to the first session can occur with a quite different type of patient. This was a very neurotic mother's guilt-ridden and obsessive good girl. She used to oblige her mother's dismissive and spiteful expectations by getting things wrong. She arrived in despair, and soon was in floods of tears. She had followed the therapist's instructions exactly and had allowed plenty of time to find the place. *"I waited for the 110 bus for a long time. Then it came. After a while I realized we were going in the opposite direction . . ."*

## The relentless healer

There is a specific technique that was developed by H. Davanloo (1978a, 1980a, 1990; see also Molnos, 1984, 1986a, 1986b) which proves that it is possible to shorten the time dramatically while doing very effective dynamic psycho-therapy. It is a technique that might be uniquely linked with the personality of its originator and might need much practising by others. However, it is worth studying it and knowing what he does, even if we cannot replicate it exactly in our work.

Davanloo manages on the one hand to maintain a warm, deeply caring and holding attitude and, at the same time, to challenge relentlessly the resistance which at first intensi-fies. He welcomes the resistance, because he knows how to turn it around into a strong therapeutic alliance. He uses the patient's growing anxiety to break through the defensive wall.

The sequence is as follows: Davanloo starts with the patient's presenting problem, makes him focus on his symptom, and explores in minute detail the circumstances in which the symptom appears. He does not accept gen-eralities, half-truths, evasion, rationalizations, vagueness, contradictions, distancing, silence, passivity, denial, ideal-ization, obsessional rumination, intellectualization. He does not interpret or explain these defences to the patient, but relentlessly questions and challenges them until all defences are exhausted (see also chapter 3).

The best way of learning to understand this technique is by studying closely the published verbatim records of his conversations with patients. For instance, one can analyse blow by blow the verbatim record of the German Architect (Davanloo, 1986) and see what the patient does, how his defensive reactions appear one after the other, how he is resisting the therapist's attempts to help him, and, finally, how the latter manages to make him look at what he is actually feeling. Another interesting verbatim record is that of the Little Blond Dutch Girl (Davanloo, 1980e; Molnos, 1986b).

Unfortunately, the patient's non-verbal communications and the therapist's voice are lost in such written records. Both are crucial elements in brief dynamic psychotherapy. The non-verbal communications reveal much about what the patient represses in himself and is unable to put into words. They serve the therapist to help the patient to get in touch with his true feelings. The art of the brief therapist includes, apart from her timing, formulations, choice of words, also the use of her voice. Words can look brusque on the printed page, while they sound warm and understanding in the actual therapy session or on a video recording. The therapist might even help to heal the split between opposite feelings by talking in a caring and warm voice while simultaneously choosing firm words that remind the patient of some harsh realities (Molnos, 1986a, p. 202).

## The therapist's attitude

Because of the many objections and prejudices against all brief forms of analytic psychotherapy and the idea that the therapist might be aggressive (chapter 1), it is necessary to spell out what attitude is actually required from the brief dynamic therapist. In part, her attitude is the same as that of any good psychotherapist, and in part it is more specific.

Any therapist's first duty, as in medicine, is, of course, not to harm the patient: *primum non nocere*. She has to do everything in the patient's best interest. To achieve this, the therapist must be aware at all times of her own great significance for the patient. Novice psychotherapists tend to underestimate how much they mean to the patient. Also, they might find it hard to understand that this great significance is to some extent loaded onto the therapist from the patient's past. To use the psychoanalytic expression, it is in the transference.

As for brief forms of analytic therapies, it is imperative to refute one particular objection—namely, that the therapist practising them is aggressive. If she is, then she herself has a problem, needs help, and should not be doing therapy at all. The challenge of the defences in brief dynamic psycho-therapy, even the strong and relentless confrontation, do not require anger or aggression, but a deeply caring deter-mination to help the patient. The challenge is directed not against the patient, but against his façade, his crippling defence system. The patient does not experience her as an attacker, but as a faithful ally. The therapist is fighting alongside the patient's healthy inner self. By doing so, she holds the patient firmly and securely all the way through. She is supporting and strengthening the patient's ego.

The therapist does not attack, does not retaliate, does not destroy, does not seduce, but neither does she collude with the patient's resistance. She accepts and respects the patient's true feelings and tries to understand his defensive moves and anxiety. Not theory, nor therapeutic perfection-ism, nor scientific curiosity, nor a self-centred need to give or to mother should override the patient's best interest or the therapist's common sense.

In short-term psychotherapy, be it brief dynamic psycho-therapy or short-term analytic group, the therapist or the group conductor cannot afford to have or harbour any of the doubts or prejudices against brief therapies described else-where (chapter 1). The therapist has to be confident and convinced that it is possible to use the limited time to max-imum effect, that good, productive work can be done within the given time limits. With her attitude and work she has to convey to the patient, or the group, that what makes a difference is not the absolute length of time, but what we do with it. This positive basic attitude towards the task is at least as important as is the therapist's technical ability to perform it. Confidence, optimism, realism and a sense of speed have to permeate the encounter. Each hour has to count.

CHAPTER THREE

# Destructive anger, healing anger, and the impulse to separate

## Overview

As we have seen, negative feelings play a crucial part in the process of BDP and are being confronted from the outset. In order to understand brief dynamic psychotherapy, it is essential to understand the role of negative feelings, emotions, and impulses—irritation, resentment, hostility, anger, hatred, rage—in normal psychic development and in close relationships, in psychic disturbances, and, of course, in the psychotherapist's work.

This chapter is based on talks I gave at the "Kossuth Lajos" University of Debrecen, Hungary, and at the annual symposium of the Dutch Association of Group Psychotherapy, in 1994. Earlier versions of these ideas were presented at the 17th London Workshop of the Group-Analytic Society (London), January 1990; and at the International Conference of Psychodrama and Analytic Group Psychotherapy, Buenos Aires, August 1985; they were published in *Group Analysis*, *19* (1986), 207–221; and 24 (1991), 133–145.

Very early on, the infant uses smiles as well as screaming, hitting, and biting to express its impulses and to obtain what it wants. "Prior to integration of the personality there is aggression. . . . At origin aggressiveness is almost synonymous with activity" (Winnicott, 1958, p. 204).

The good-enough mother tries to provide what the infant needs, but she instinctively leaves a time-lag, and progressively increases it, between the demands and their satisfaction. Faced with expressions of infantile rage, she waits a while, then she contains the rage gently but firmly. Her fundamentally warm, loving attitude remains in place whatever the infant does, and even when she herself experiences irritation, annoyance, or anger. She never retaliates, never takes revenge on her child. Her basic attitude overrides any mistake she makes and is bound to make.

The not–good-enough mother is likely to be someone who has been emotionally wounded in her own childhood. She might be afraid of any anger or unable to control her own anger, or she might have been depressed, in which case her own infantile rage might have been driven underground, deeply buried, and turned against her inner self. Depending on the type of problem she has with negative feelings and impulses, she might try to feed the baby on demand, satisfy its every need on the spot and without any delay, or, conversely, impose a far too rigid regime, or behave erratically, or be punitive or violent or cold and rejecting in dealing with her infant.

In some families there is physical violence or verbal and other abuse, or all these together. Other families go out of their way to avoid any unpleasant topics or actions, any expression of negative feelings, and sweep every problem under the carpet. Both categories of families have failed to keep their positive and negative feelings together. They have failed to sort out in a constructive way the differences that exist among family members. Both types have unresolved problems with anger, and both damage their children. The first type of family is likely to hurt the child with acts of rejection and by disregarding its need for love and attachment. The second type of family might deny not only the negative feelings—their own and the child's—but also the child's need to separate and grow, thus frustrating what I call the "impulse to separate".

Not only in the family, but in any human group—at the work place, in the club, the sports team, a professional association, learned society, and so on—there can be and are problems with closeness, separateness, and anger. The question of how we handle anger, in ourselves and in our dealings with others, has obvious implications for larger social phenomena, such as political and religious movements as well as the violence and generally destructive behaviour of the human animal today.

There are misconceptions about anger in society at large and also among some therapists who practise ideologically motivated forms of treatment or counselling. Most misconceptions derive from the simple belief that love is always a good thing and hate always bad. This is, of course, a false dichotomy, because love and hatred belong together and can only be separated at our peril. Both can be good or bad. It depends on where, towards whom or what they are directed, when and how they are expressed. Also, as in other animals, love (which holds, protects, nourishes) and hate (which chases away, restrains, rejects) stand together in the service of the preservation of the individual and the conservation of the species.

One of the main tasks of all analytic psychotherapists is to monitor hostile feelings in the here-and-now, making sure that they do not get swept under the carpet and/or acted-out. If underlying hostile feelings and acting-out against the boundaries go unchallenged, they will end up by destroying the therapy itself. Positive feelings are more easily expressed and therefore cause fewer problems and need less of the therapist's attention. However, positive feelings that are too intense and inappropriately so—for instance, when the patient "falls in love" with the therapist—are on the whole a form of acting out of destructive impulses and should be treated as such. They cannot be viewed as just positive feelings.

In this chapter I want to outline my distinction between two kinds of anger—"healing anger" and the "destructive anger"—alongside the concept of "destructive idealization", as well as the notion of the "impulse to separate". These concepts are essential for understanding the core of analytic psychotherapy, and of brief dynamic psychotherapy in particular.

## What is destructive anger?

EXAMPLE 14: *destructive anger*

A young man who worked near a tropical forest used to tame wildcat kittens in his spare time. One of the kittens scratched him, then scratched him again. When it scratched him a third time, the man seized the kitten in a sudden fit of hatred and, barely able to withstand his impulse to squeeze that tiny neck in his hand, hurled the kitten far away into the bush. That was destructive fury against something he had loved. He took out his rage on a wild kitten who did not know better and would certainly not mend its ways because of such violent treatment. The experience left the young man feeling bad about himself. He told the therapist this story twenty years later and added: "I got very depressed afterwards. It could have been a child. I don't know what got over me." Yet, his unconscious did know. There was, indeed, a direct link with a child. His younger brother bore a scar on his forehead from the age of 4, when he fell down on a stone-strewn path. The patient remembered: "We were walking together. I put out my foot in front of him, and he tripped over it. I did not feel anything. I don't know why I did it. I think I was vaguely curious to see what would happen." In the end he acknowledged his hatred of his younger brother, who had become his mother's favourite after their father died. From then on his life had turned to misery. He had felt completely rejected, excluded, and alone.

Let us define "destructive anger" as follows. It is the anger that:

1. is expressed at the wrong time, usually too late;
2. is displaced towards someone or something other than the person who provoked it; and/or
3. comes to be connected with a cover-up issue, not with that which triggered it off.

The example of the wild kitten has all three ingredients: (1) the young man's rage was expressed some fifteen years too late; (2) it had been transferred successively from his beloved father (who, by suddenly dying, abandoned him) and from his mother (who rejected him in favour of her other son) first onto the brother and, finally, onto the wild kitten; (3) furthermore, the rage became connected to a cover-up issue: to scratches rather than to the hurt he felt because his love and care for the kitten had been rejected.

## A hidden manifestation of destructive anger: acting out

Perhaps the most dangerous form of "destructive anger" is one that is not experienced at all as anger or any feeling, but is acted out instead. That is what happened to the tamer of wild kittens when at the age of 7, without feeling anything or knowing why, he put out his foot in front of his toddler brother.

The repressed, unrecognized, destructive anger can turn also against the self and appear in many different disguises. The patient might suffer from psychosomatic symptoms, become accident-prone, attempt suicide, or commit unconscious acts of self-sabotage in relationships, in his work, and so on.

The repressed, destructive anger primarily directed against the self is bound to affect others as well. It is enough to think of the havoc caused to their families by anorexics or drug-addicts. Self-destructive anger mars all sorts of relationships. In therapy, the patient whose unconscious destructive rage is primarily directed against himself in the form of passive-resistant reactions, stalemated silences, recurrent psychosomatic symptoms, and so on can end up by defeating the therapist or the therapy group in their desire to help.

Equally, the destructive anger against others always ends up by being damaging to the self also. The tamer of wild kittens, for instance, became depressed after his destructive act, and he similarly remained deeply unhappy after the breakdown of each of his many stormy relationships with women.

## Destructive idealization as a form of acting out

I would like to introduce here the concept of "destructive idealization" (Molnos, 1991) as a particularly insidious way of acting out the destructive anger. Extreme animal fear or archaic fear in the deep unconscious produces a primitive split of impulses leading to the idealization of one object and, as a result, hatred of the other. This whole process is what I call "destructive idealization".

Idealization, by which someone loses touch with the reality of the idealized object, is invariably destructive in the long run. I consider it a form of acting out of destructive anger, because the latter remains totally unconscious and fuels the idealization that persists.

Sometimes the therapeutic dyad, or, in group therapy, the group-as-a-whole, is overidealized at the expense of the rest of the world. One of the dangers for the novice psychotherapist or group analyst is that she might be taken in by this seductive state of affairs and, instead of confronting the patient, collude with the flattering idealization. In more technical terms, she might develop an inappropriate positive countertransference.

In long-term individual therapy, the classic analytic situation, the absence of an identifiable task or focus creates anxiety and, therefore, internal pressure. Positive feelings easily split from negative ones.

The severely damaged patient, like the baby, cannot tolerate that its mother—that is to say, the therapist—is good and bad at the same time. For fear of losing her, for fear of destroying her with his own rage and omnipotent destructive fantasies, the patient tends to overidealize the therapist. As time goes by and the patient gains confidence, hopefully a more balanced and realistic appreciation will replace the one-sided positive image. The patient whose damage is so early that he cannot tolerate his own emotional ambivalence when confronted with it needs to be held for a while before the split can be healed. In other words, he needs a relatively longer therapy.

The process of destructive idealization can be observed outside therapy as well.

For instance, it appears as a result of the archaic fear and anxiety around HIV/AIDS (Molnos, 1990). Carers often overidealize the AIDS patient, whose wretched condition and whole being may acquire a numinous, transcendental quality in the eyes of the projector. The idealization is often reciprocated. The necessary boundaries between the carers and the patients break down. Negative feelings are split off and projected elsewhere, an exalted atmosphere of self-sacrificing and excluding love develops on the AIDS ward, followed by confusion and at times by total chaos. Phenomena of destructive idealization and confusion could be observed in the late 1980s in a variety of AIDS-related contexts—at managerial, national, and international levels, where HIV/AIDS policies had to be developed, decided upon, and translated into action programmes.

The powerful defence against an intolerable present, against the here-and-now, can lead to losing contact with reality. The abhorred part of reality is eliminated from the mind, and the longed-for condition is idealized in fantasy.

It is generally true that the human mind, once the here-and-now becomes intolerably frightening or painful, escapes into another time, another place, and idealizes it—a process in which the splitting of positive and negative feelings is inherent. One way very old people can deal with the lack of a future and the bleakness of the present is by casting their mind into the past and enjoying it in fantasy, overidealizing it.

The future can also be overidealized. Painfully negative and conflictual feelings attached to the past can be dealt with by obliterating in one's memory the past itself. We know what it means if a patient is surprised by the detailed childhood recollections of other group members and says: "I don't like to talk about the past. I hardly remember it anyway. I have always lived in the future."

By splitting off the past, we cut ourselves loose from our roots and start drifting. Then we begin to project into the future what we have lost or never had. What is longed for, but forever unreachable, is overidealized because the desire is too strong to bear the recognition that we will never have it.

The fundamentalist blows up buildings, kills and maims in the name of an idealized future, and disregards the reality of the destruction and sufferings his actions cause. A dictator, a self-appointed secular god, bulldozes ancient villages and orders torture and genocide to create a "*tabula rasa*"—a clean slate—on which to construct his personal version of utopia. Both the fundamentalist and the dictator hate and destroy the past and are obsessed with the future and idealize it. They are victims of a primitive split.

The often concealed yet ever-present theme of *tabula rasa* reveals the link existing between utopias and violence and destruction.

### An overt manifestation of destructive anger:
### universal rage

Some patients are overtly hostile and have no difficulty whatsoever in expressing anger against the therapist or other members in a group. The patient keeps on raging against the therapist, like forever having recurrent temper tantrums. He accuses her of all sorts of sins she has not committed. His anger is unremitting, repetitive, and unpleasant to experience, and does not seem to lead anywhere. He throws back whatever is said at the very person who tries to help him. It is a demanding anger, that of a baby who wants something it does not get. It is shaking with impotent rage. The rage is meant to punish the therapist for not satisfying his need. Somewhere there is a lurking fantasy that if the therapist could be eliminated altogether, there would be release from the despair.

A combination of strong need and helplessness produces that rage. Thoughts accompanying the rage might be critical of the therapist, and negative in the extreme. However, underneath there is the impulse to come closer to the therapist. The rage is about feeling pushed away. The rage is against the unattainable object of one's need and against the need itself. This type of anger is destructive. It is an anger that has little to do with the here-and-now where it is expressed. It is used in the here-and-now as a defence against other feelings such as pain, sadness, helplessness, and so on.

This universal rage can be said to be "in the transference", or it can be called "negative transference", or, in some cases, even "negative therapeutic reaction" (Seinfeld, 1990). As the barrage of negative outbursts is unremitting and unrelated to the reality of the therapist's actual behaviour, it is clear that such a constant attitude is the manifestation of a pattern from the patient's past. Moreover, it appears with other people as well. In fact, I call it "universal rage" to indicate that it is there all the time on the lookout, waiting for anyone and anything to become attached to.

Such a person tends to find it extremely difficult to separate from anyone important to him and finds it very difficult to accept that one day his therapy has to finish. So important is the issue of separation that one could say that the therapist who has not helped the patient to separate from her has not helped him at all. The first step is to help him to stop hiding behind his constant anger and start getting in touch with his true feelings and vulnerability.

The pre-condition that enables one to show one's vulnerability under the defiant surface as well as to express one's anger with the most needed, loved, hated, and feared person is that one should feel safe enough to do so. Only if it is "safe-enough" can the patient express his negative or hostile feelings with a sufficient degree of immediacy and openness. How the therapist facilitates a safe, open, and tolerant environment is amply described in the literature. Here it suffices to point out a very important though uncomfortable task incumbent on the therapist: she has to make sure that no hostility against her is deflected by the patient towards other persons—previous therapists, the patient's partner, relatives, friends, colleagues—nor that it remains suppressed for too long.

The therapist has to ensure constantly that any furious tirades against others out there—the partner, the mother, the neighbour, the boss, the organization where the patient works or where the therapy is taking place, and so on—be quickly recognized as belonging to the here-and-now. The denied anger towards the therapist has to be brought into the open and transformed into "healing anger".

Failure to bring the hostility, the suppressed, denied, or displaced anger against the therapist out into the open can lead to the patient's destructive acting-out against others and against the therapeutic boundaries and to the whole therapeutic process disintegrating. Moreover, this failure to confront the patient's hostility naturally leads to the rise of hostile feelings in the therapist herself or, to put it more technically, to difficulties with her countertransference. In brief dynamic psychotherapy all this is prevented by the highly active therapist who starts the whole process by confronting the negative feelings in the here-and-now and dealing with them at the start.

## Origin of destructive anger
## and destructive idealization

The roots of both destructive anger and destructive idealization are in the mechanism of splitting. We may use the
phraseology of Klein (1955, p. 143) and say that at the
initial, unintegrated stage of psychic development "splitting
is at its height and persecutory anxiety predominates".
Klein explained the splitting of the object into a "good" and a
"bad" object as the earliest, most primitive kind of defence
against anxiety, especially in the paranoid–schizoid position, in the first three or four months of life, when it affects
the perception of part-objects.

Extreme feelings and the failure to integrate them can
be seen also as a basic fault in the personality. Balint described some particularly difficult patients escaping into
overidealizations: ". . . fantasies about a perfect partner, or of
perfect harmony with their whole environment, perfect un-
troubled happiness, perfect contentment with themselves
and with their world, and so on . . ." (Balint, 1968, pp. 88–
89). He attributed these fantasies to a flaw in the basic
structure of the personality, something he came to call the
"basic fault". Balint also pointed out that the introjection, in
idealized form, of a previously hated and persecuted object,
as in some conversions, may result in intolerance, sectari-
anism, and apostolic fury. He writes: ". . . the ambivalently
loved and idealized, introjected image must be preserved at
all costs as a good and whole internal object. In such a state
any outside criticism—whether justified or unfounded—
merely mobilises all the forces of the pent-up hatred and
aggressiveness against the critic . . ." (Balint, 1952, pp. 282–
283).

In her essay on "The Archaic Matrix of the Oedipus Complex and Utopia", Chasseguet-Smirgel (1986) proposes a
psychoanalytic explanation of what I call the "destructive
idealization" of the future as reflected in utopias. She writes:
". . . there is a primary wish to rediscover a universe without
obstacles, a smooth maternal belly, stripped of its contents,
to which free access is desired. . . . there is no question of a

stage of the Oedipus complex, but of the representation of a mode of mental functioning without hindrances, ruled by the pleasure principle" (pp. 92–93).

Among the dominant utopic themes, Chasseguet-Smirgel pinpoints that of the *tabula rasa*. To build Utopia, one first has to level the past to the ground. Utopia can be built only on a smooth surface, with no memory, no remembrance, not even scars left. This theme of *tabula rasa,* which can only be achieved by complete annihilation of what went before, shows best just how destructive idealization can be.

## *Splitting of feelings and the failure to separate*

As long as opposite feelings are kept separate, the person tends to idealize and to identify or merge with the idealized other person, ideology, or fetish. He cannot be himself: he clings to the person with whom he is unconditionally, blindly in love, or to his ideology, or to his fixed ideas. He clings to the therapist and cannot separate from her. All of a sudden he might find himself loving someone else, believing in the opposite ideology, clinging to another person instead of the therapist. The objects of his idealization have changed. Actually, nothing has changed. He is still unable to be a separate individual and, by the same token, unable to relate.

Splitting is defined as an unconscious process by which positive and negative impulses and feelings that are too difficult to be held together spring apart and become projected onto different people. The clear split between good and bad relieves the anxiety of doubt in the toddler's world. "Daddy is bad; Mummy is nice." . . . "I love Mummy, I don't like Daddy."

Parents are the first targets for the projection of our polarized feelings and passions. Other relatives, playmates, pets, dolls, friends, neighbours, office colleagues, and so on follow. Their real selves can be obscured from and by the projector in different ways. We might unload a revolting mess from the past onto the projection target. That sets the scene for destructive anger. Often, however, the luggage we cannot bear to own and carry contains the best parts of ourselves. Such denied aspects of ourselves become wonderful and precious ornaments, the beautiful clothes with which we dress others up. Since it obscures the reality of the other, this idealizing projection leads to destruction too.

The process of becoming a separate individual is both rewarding and painful. If there is not good-enough mothering, the child might rebel prematurely, before it is ready. Without a protective and nurturing psychic environment, the child develops a false façade of independence and separateness. And the vulnerability underneath it all remains and deepens. Another possibility is that the infant might tend to perpetuate the dependent state of affairs with the not–good-enough parent, to cling and make itself more helpless than it is. As the child grows up, it will increasingly resent the very person to whom it clings, whoever it might be. The much-needed person is experienced as the oppressor, yet the fear of being rejected or abandoned is far too great to show the anger. The anger is lived out in fantasies that generate guilt, submissive behaviour, and more anger. That is the beginning of the downwards spiral.

Studies in animal behaviour have shown that adult individuals of the same species maintain a prescribed "individual distance" (Hediger, 1955) from each other when travelling together. Among humans, the physical distance at which people are comfortable when they talk to each other varies from culture to culture (Hall, 1959, p. 164). If such specific distances are reduced, there is an immediate impulse to separate. When the separation is hindered, irritation and anger will follow. In persistently overcrowded conditions that anger might become murderous rage.

I believe there is a particular type of anger that arises because the impulse to separate has been frustrated. This anger is directed towards the most needed person (= therapist, loved person, mother). In most patients this impulse has been inhibited (split off, repressed, avoided, denied, displaced, converted, etc.).

There is also a psychic "individual distance" that is necessary for a balanced and workable relationship with one's nearest and dearest. It is the healthy distance not from one's enemy or one's neighbour, but from the very person to whom one is closest. It is the intrapsychic distance, a mental independence from the most needed person. It is the distance that is missing in a symbiotic relationship. If we fail to separate from and maintain some internal distance to the person we love, we end up by no longer loving but resenting and hating that person.

As analytic psychotherapists we firmly believe in the necessity of boundaries—boundaries that hold the whole spectrum of emotions together from one extreme to the other, boundaries that allow us to conjure the past into the present and work through it in the here-and-now. All analytic therapies—whether short-term or long-term, open-ended individual therapy or group therapy conducted along analytic lines—are designed to explore and tolerate emotional ambivalence. The healing emotional experience consists in discovering that each of us, and our relationships—be it the therapeutic or any other relationship—become stronger once we stop splitting the positive from the negative, once we stop unconsciously overidealizing.

For the sake of psychic health, opposite feelings have to be kept together in struggle and in harmony.

### Healing anger

The opposite of "destructive anger" is the "healthy","normal" anger, which I call "healing anger", a concept akin to Malan's "constructive aggression" (1979, p. 96). The notion of "healing anger" seems to be more useful because of its immediate link with therapy itself as well as with good, everyday relationships. It is anger that liberates, clears the air, and brings people closer together. In psychotherapy it produces positive shifts.

The following example is taken from the first session of a therapy with a woman of 52—we shall call her Mavis—complaining of deep depression to the point of not being able to perform the simplest daily chores.

### EXAMPLE 15: *healing anger*

Mavis looked monumental as she arrived clad in a dowdy dress of nondescript colour. On her big white face there was resentment and a strained smile of social obligation. She launched into complaints about her husband, Harry, a dull man only interested in his work. He was no fun. Mavis spoke dispassiona.ely, with an air of intellectual and moral superiority. Her voice sounded self-righteous and domineering. For some reason she started obsessing about holidays. The therapist interrupted to find out the last time she did feel all right. She said it was eighteen months ago. "Harry and I had a lovely holiday in Greece." After that holiday she had a rash all over her body. Now she felt worthless, useless. She could not cope; she often cried, had panic attacks, and lived on tranquillizers. "I cannot take any more", Mavis said. She declared that it was all physical. It had to do with the menopause. Her doctor said it was depression . . . a virus she picked up on that holiday in Greece. . . . Each time the therapist challenged her, a barrage of words about symptoms followed. The list of possible physical causes grew. Finally the therapist said calmly, "If you feel that your problem is purely physical, I cannot help you. I am not a medical doctor. In that case, you ought to see a medical specialist." The patient instantaneously burst out crying. Then she stopped abruptly and, now fully in control of herself, turned against the therapist and told her in no uncertain

terms: "You made me cry, you forced me to cry!"
Although that was not quite accurate, the therapist said
nothing but let her go on expressing her anger. For a
moment she had hated the therapist for "making" her
cry. "I always hated losing control", she added. After
that, there was a totally changed atmosphere. Mavis
talked about her cold and strict mother; her parents'
divorce; her half-sister; her own marriage to the wrong
man, Harry . . . Past events unfolded in vivid pictures.
The following session she arrived smartly dressed,
announcing proudly that her doctor had agreed to stop
her anti-depressants. She was free of her symptoms at
the time of the ninth session, and her therapy was
successfully terminated after the sixteenth session.

"Healing anger" is the one that is clearly experienced and
adequately expressed:

1.  at the right time, possibly at the time when it arises;
2.  towards the person who provoked it;
3.  and connected with the real issue that triggered it off.

In order to meet these three conditions, there should not
be any overload of hostile feelings from the past towards the
person who provoked the anger, nor any hostile feelings
unconsciously transferred from other persons or from other
situations. As for the adequate expression of the anger in
the here-and-now, that will greatly depend on the circumstances, the environment, and the culture in which the
interaction takes place.
    It is possible to argue that the three conditions of the
"healing anger" as stated above can never be met. In fact,
there always will be some residual hostility from the past or
transferred from somewhere else that will cloud this stated
ideal of "healthy" or "healing" anger. Nevertheless, it is worth
stating the ideal in order to contrast it with its opposite—the
"destructive anger". Apart from some extreme psychotic con-

ditions, sheer, undiluted "destructive anger" is also a mere abstraction. Even the sudden rage of the tamer of wildcats had a base in the there-and-then reality. After all, the kitten did scratch him. The value of these abstractions consists in signposting two extremes. Between them lies a whole gamut of manifestations of anger, from those that clear the air to those that poison it further.

The example shows how "healing anger" arises under pressure exerted by the therapist who confronts the defences. It also shows that this confrontation is completely non-aggressive, though it has to be incisive and to the point.

In this example the therapist did not accept the patient's many physical complaints as being her main problem, but treated them as her way of defending herself against her true feelings and anxieties in the relationship with her husband (DAX/C).

Mavis suffered from incapacitating psychosomatic symptoms. Those symptoms turned out to be her unconscious defensive compromise (DC) between her accumulated rage against her husband (–XC) and the fear (AC) of losing him, being totally rejected, and being abandoned by him if she were to express that rage.

The therapist put the responsibility back on the patient to decide whether she preferred to carry on using those defences or was prepared to look deeper into herself. Mavis's first outburst of crying was a sudden response to feeling rejected. That feeling actually came from her painful childhood (–XP), streaming into the here-and-now like a tidal wave. She was an intelligent woman, and it took her only seconds to realize that this did not belong to the here-and-now. Immediately thereafter she experienced and expressed real anger with the therapist (–XT) who had disrupted her defences. That anger was "healing anger" not because it was strong, but because it was experienced and expressed (1) as soon as it arose; (2) towards the therapist who had provoked it; and (3) on the issue that triggered it off—namely, in her perception, "being forced to lose control".

### Breaking through the "wall":
### healing anger and the impulse to separate

Sooner or later in the therapy all good analytic psychotherapists deal with the patient's anger. However, the "relentless healer" (chapter 2) does it straight away, right at the start, and he does it in a particular way. This is a specific sequence, which is the core of his technique and its hallmark (Davanloo, 1990, pp. 217–282). It is shown in Figure 9. This sequence is repeated again and again in the course of the therapy, whenever the patient's resistance blocks the work.

The notation is that of the four triangles (Figure 7). The symbol D (= defence) after the term "resistance" in the sequence is shorthand for saying that the patient resists the therapist's attempt to get at the true feeling and that this resistance activates one after the other ($D_1$, $D_2$, . . ., $D_n$) the patient's customary defences in the psychoanalytic sense of the term "defence". (For the original Freudian distinction between *Widerstand* [= resistance] and *Abwehr* [= defence], see Laplanche & Pontalis, 1973, pp. 394–397, 103–107. See also Figure 10.) As a result of this relentless confrontation of the defences, the patient's resistance to look at his true feelings in relation to the presenting problem (DC) switches to become resistance in the here-and-now (DT), which the therapist continues to challenge until all defences are exhausted. Sometimes this same sequence starts with the therapist pro   ig for true feelings within a past relationship (XP), and the   .ie sequence goes on as above ($D_1P$, $D_2P$, . . ., $D_nP$).

The best opportunity to bring out the anger in the here-and-now is at the start of the therapy, when both the need for the therapist's help and the determination to change are strong, and the patient's unconscious has not yet learned to out-manoeuvre the therapist's particular approach.

In this technique the strong but fair challenge is combined with a completely secure "psychic holding". Contrary to what happens in long-term, open-ended psychotherapy in which there is first "holding" and then confronting, in this technique there is no time-lag between the two. Holding

| THERAPIST | PATIENT |
|---|---|
| Probes for the true feeling re current problem (XC) | $\rightarrow$ First resistance ($D_1C$) $\rightarrow$ |
| $\rightarrow$ Challenges first resistance ($D_1C$) | $\rightarrow$ Resistance ($D_2C$) $\rightarrow$ |
| $\rightarrow$ Challenges resistance ($D_2C$) | $\rightarrow$ Resistance ($D_nC$) $\rightarrow$ |
| $\rightarrow$ Challenges resistance ($D_nC$) | $\rightarrow$ Activation of the anger with the therapist (−XT) and resistance against acknowledging and expressing this anger ($D_1T$) $\rightarrow$ |
| $\rightarrow$ Challenges resistance ($D_1T$) | $\rightarrow$ Resistance ($D_2T$) $\rightarrow$ |
| $\rightarrow$ Challenges resistance ($D_2T$) | $\rightarrow$ Resistance ($D_nT$) $\rightarrow$ |
| | $\rightarrow$ Expresses and acknowledges his *anger* with the therapist (−XT) |
| | $\rightarrow$ *relief* and warm feelings (+XT) |
| | $\rightarrow$ relevant material, expression of true feelings (XC and/or XP) $\rightarrow$ TCP-link |
| | $\rightarrow$ a new cycle. |

FIGURE 9. The sequence of H. Davanloo's confronting technique

the patient and confronting him happen simultaneously. This combination of holding and relentless challenge enables the patient to experience and express his anger in the here-and-now.

The moment when the patient is suddenly in touch with his anger against the much-needed therapist and expresses it has a magic, liberating quality. It is a moment of separation within a good relationship. The anger is "in self-defence", so to speak, because the therapist has disrupted the neurotic resistance. It is not anger in the transference. It is real anger, very much in the here-and-now. This healing anger is related directly to the therapist's actual behaviour. The patient might never have expressed before, or even felt, his anger within a good relationship.

**General observations:** "Defence" is a central and essential operational concept in psychotherapy. However, the theory of defence mechanisms is not very clear or consistent. In principle any psychic operation or feeling or behaviour or action can be used by the unconscious as a defence against being cornered, uncovered.

Perhaps the simplest and the most important defence mechanism is **r e p r e s s i o n**. It constitutes the basis in the formation of the unconscious and is often the starting point in more complex defensive processes. The initial resistance, which is encountered in all psychotherapy, manifests itself in the patient using his habitual defensive moves. Although each of us has his/her own uniquely personal defensive style, some of the underlying defence mechanisms are more characteristic of one pathology than another, e.g. borderline disorders (b), hysteria (h), mania (m), narcissism (n), obsession (o), paranoia (p).

None of the following five lists is complete. There are also overlappings between the various groupings. E.g. intellectualization can appear in the form of unspoken thoughts, i.e. as an intrapsychic response, or it can be verbalized, i.e. be a verbal manifestation of an internal defensive response.

**Defence mechanisms** (described by S. Freud, Anna Freud, Melanie Klein, and others): repression (h), turning round upon the subject's own self, reversal into the opposite, conversion (h), substitution (o), projection (p), regression, reaction-formation, isolation of affect (o), undoing (o), introjection, sublimation, denial in fantasy, idealization, identification with the aggressor, incorporation (m). Primitive defences (described by Melanie Klein): splitting of the object (b), projective identification (b), denial of psychic reality, omnipotent control over objects.

FIGURE 10.

It therefore seems rather questionable that this real anger should be regarded as "anger in the transference", as it is sometimes called. The patient has not gone through a prolonged and difficult period of "negative transference", negativity, and rage. He simply turns around and stands his ground against the therapist. It is "healing anger", and it

**Defensive responses** (intrapsychic): repression (h), suppression, denial (h) / disavowal, avoidance (h), constriction (h), conversion/ somatization (h), rapid shifts in affect (b), regression, reversal into the opposite feeling, turning round upon the subject's own self, introjection (h), incorporation, sublimation, cutting off feeling, shallow affect, isolation, undoing, substitution, reaction formation, intellectualization (o), intellectual insight (o), obsessional rumination, displacement, blocking memory, shifting self-concepts (h), externalization of blame (n), etc.

**Defensive reactions** (interpersonal): distancing, passivity, obstinacy, defiance, idealization, attempts at role reversal, not hearing, not understanding, identification with the aggressor, projection, acting out feelings towards the therapist and/or towards others, etc.

**Non-verbal manifestations of defensive responses** (to be monitored by the therapist): silence, avoiding a relevant topic, sudden change of subject, verbal content at odds with the quality of the voice, avoiding eye contact, regressive weeping, gestures, grimaces, blushing, changing position in the chair, tics, psychosomatic symptoms, attacks on the implicitly and/or explicitly agreed boundaries (e.g. late-coming, arriving too early, "forgetting" appointment), etc.

**Verbal manifestations of defensive reactions** (mostly "tactical" to be closely monitored by the therapist): half-truths, generalizations, vagueness, evasiveness, rationalizations (o), contradictions (between statements; between verbal content and non-verbal signals); short-circuiting (h), social discourse (h), compulsive talking (o), "story-telling" as covert struggle to control topics (o), etc.

Defences: types and categories

seems to be the patient's reaction to having to give up the resistance. It appears at once after an intense period of resistance, after having used up all the habitual defences. It is a sudden turning-around against the therapist not in order to destroy her, but in order to reset the distance with her. The patient's anger is saying: "Stop. That's enough.

Although you are right, although you are doing it for me, I don't want you to go any further! Here is me. Stop shaking me, I am not a lump of jelly. I am I. You have to respect me. And please help me. I will co-operate. I need you." Then they can start working together.

At the beginning of this process, as the therapist confronts the patient with his defences one after the other, very soon the "wall goes up". This is not just a figure of speech, but a real experience. The same description is given by speakers of other languages. "*Una muralla se levanta en mî*" ["A wall is rising in me"], said a Spanish patient. "I don"t dare to come out from behind the wall" . . . "There is a wall of anger in me" . . . "I would like to get rid of this wall" . . . "It's as though I can only bring myself to peep over the wall, but I cannot leave it altogether", and so on are phrases used by patients. The wall can be of glass: "I am surrounded by armour-plated glass" . . . "I am sitting in a thick glass bubble." The imagery may be slightly different—but, interestingly, not much. So, one hears, for example, that "The shutters come down" . . . "I had to pull up the drawbridge", or "I had to retreat into my shell". In all these cases the patient is inside his fortress, the protected area, and the therapist is outside.

In all these cases the defence is against being "overrun", "invaded", "taken over". This is what many patients have experienced their parents doing. They prevented a normal, progressive separation. The child's healthy reaction was to "close-up", to "put up a wall, a barrier" inside himself. A teenager, dreading his mother's intrusion and control, puts up a sign saying "Private" on his bedroom door. The seductive, inconsistent parent, the absent parent, or the outright neglectful or cruel parent also teaches the child to "put up a wall". In order to minimize the pain, the child quickly learns to "put up a wall" between himself and such a not–good-enough parent. All these premature separations solidify as neurotic defensive patterns in later life. That is why the therapist has to help the patient to demolish the wall first to recover the lost true feelings of pain, anger, warmth, affection, sadness, and joy, and then to learn to separate in a healthy, modulated, non-compulsive way.

The quality of the anger that appears on first breaking through the defensive wall is neither remarkably strong, nor is it persistent. In most cases its expression is brief, restrained, non-dramatic, neither aggressive nor over the top. The anger acquires a healing quality when it finds its expression in a calm, incisive manner by dealing with the person and the issue that provoked it and near to the time when the hurt occurred.

Its strength does not bear a direct relation to its healing power or positive "mutative" effect. The healing effect comes from the precision with which it is directed to the right target, on the right issue, and at the right time. The "mutative", healing anger expresses the impulse to separate, not the wish to merge, to punish, to retaliate, or to destroy.

In the therapeutic situation not all freely expressed anger is, of course, "healing anger". We recognize the expression of "healing anger" by its remarkable and immediate "mutative" effect. It is usually followed by a feeling of great relief. Other feelings—such as sadness, warmth, and gratitude—surface. There is an immediate positive change in the atmosphere. The patient becomes lively and spontaneous. All of a sudden, the therapeutic alliance becomes strong, and the unconscious starts pouring out a flood of new material.

After having expressed his anger against the therapist, the patient becomes his separated, individual self and no longer uses half his mind to gauge what the therapist expects him to say or feel. The patient is himself, the "hidden dependence" (Molnos, 1980) is lifted; he can speak his mind and express his feelings with immediacy and without fear.

As mentioned before, immediately after the "healing anger" positive feelings (+XT) appear; the current (DAX/C) and past (DAX/P) conflicts are linked with the one in the here-and-now (DAX/T). These so-called TCP-links are repeated many times and in many variations in the subsequent course of the therapy.

An environment that is safe enough to allow the expression of negative feelings against the very person on whom we most depend is an eminently healing environment. In the analytic situation this person is the therapist. "Safe-enough", of course, means not only that she will not retaliate, but also that she will help the patient to tolerate the existence and expression of hostility against her in the here-and-now, to talk about such feelings freely as they appear, and to understand their connections with anxieties and defences within the therapeutic relationship and relationships outside (TCP-links).

"Destructive anger", whatever form it takes and no matter how irremovable it appears, can be transformed into something more constructive. Overcoming "destructive anger" and facilitating "healing anger" is essential to the practice of BDP, and it also forms part of the process of any successful dynamic therapy, be it long- or short-term, individual or group therapy.

# CHAPTER FOUR

# Final, intermediate, and immediate aims of brief and other analytic psychotherapies

## *The therapist's neutrality*

When a patient makes atheistic statements, ridicules religious devotion, or shows total disregard for other people's sensitivities and suffering, I have to watch myself. I have to remind myself that my task is to help him to discover himself by himself, regardless of what I think of his ideas and his attitudes towards the world, regardless of my own beliefs.

Actually, I do believe in God's existence. Having gone through a short atheistic spell in my teens, I then came to think that the atheistic position is untenable. Even in

---

This chapter is based mainly on a seminar I gave to Ph.D. students at the "Kossuth Lajos" University, Debrecen, Hungary, in September 1994. I had also given a talk on the same topic at a conference of the Association of Pastoral Care and Counselling, held in Pinner, Middlesex, England, in May 1986.

periods of faithless apathy, I feel that a God does exist, and I have simply lost contact with him.

My faith in life is unwaveringly constant. Life for me remains a gift, even in moments of suffering. It is better to endure pain than not to be. Only very briefly, once, or perhaps twice, have I thought the other way around. We human beings do a great deal to spoil that gift in us and in others. This overwhelming belief in the value of life undoubtedly influences my dealings with patients and is bound to affect them, I hope, in a positive, constructive way. On the other hand, the fact that I happen to be a Christian and a Catholic does not have much specific bearing on my work. Most of my patients are non-believers or belong to other denominations or to non-Christian churches. Fortunately, this divergence does not cause any conflict in me.

I have been influenced not only by certain basic human and Christian values, but also by the living history of my people, their immense suffering over many centuries, which in some areas continues even today. Both influences are interlinked (Molnos, 1992).

As a Hungarian-born third-generation refugee, I am particularly sensitive to the abuse of power, to oppression, to ethnic prejudice and discrimination. I hate the cruelty against those who are vulnerable, the torture and the persecution of the defenceless. I am a fervent believer in a democratic system of government and the individual's freedom balanced by self-restraint and personal responsibility. I loathe blind fanaticisms and dictatorships, left and right. Even more, I loathe those who play with high moral values by using the language of idealism to disguise their true aims and deceive the innocent, as too often happened in the name of Communism during the occupation of Eastern Europe by Russia from 1945 to 1989.

Although I do not disclose to patients my religion, my politics, or any other aspects of my life or beliefs, my values do influence the kind of therapist I am.

There is no such thing as a perfectly neutral, objective, unbiased psychotherapist. We all are influenced by the attitudes and values in the midst of which we live and have grown up. As one's value system operates mostly on an unconscious level, a psychotherapist must make a deliberate effort to become fully aware of it.

None of us is able to avoid being guided by ideals and by value judgements, implicit or explicit, about ourselves and others. Both the patient and the therapist are guided all the time by value judgements, by, indeed, moral judgements about each other and about themselves. Problems arise when the therapist, who has the responsibility of the total therapeutic situation, does not know that this is so or does not want to know it.

What the therapist cannot afford is to have unmonitored unconscious aims of her own. It is her responsibility to become as fully aware as possible of the personal, theoretical, and ideological biases that might influence her professional functioning. It is up to her to protect the therapeutic situation and her relationship with the patient from undue interferences, including from her own particular biases.

## Perfection:
### neurotic goal or guiding ideal

Therapeutic perfectionism is one of the secondary causes of ever longer therapies (chapter 1, Figure 2). Striving for a perfect outcome is a neurotic goal in psychotherapy in which the patient or the therapist or both can be trapped.

Idealized conceptions of mental health and ideas of perfection can become the seductive guiding fantasy in psychotherapy (Appelbaum, 1981, p. 161). When the therapist succumbs to the lure of perfection, she gives up her professional stance. The unrealistic striving towards a perfect therapeutic outcome might be due to fantasies of wanting to be better than other therapists or simply the wish to explore how good a therapist one is, how far it is possible to succeed. The therapist might miss the optimal time to finish a particular therapy because of her personal dissatisfaction with what has been already achieved.

Some patients start therapy with the half-conscious expectation that at the end of it they will emerge as a brand-new person, free from all problems and internal struggles. Such images of perfection are static, and therefore they constitute not only an unrealistic but also a most undesirable aim.

Perfectionism can be an obsessional defence against guilt. Striving for it is some patients' neurotic attempt to protect themselves against being put down, feeling vulnerable, and hurt, against the consequent upsurge of impotent rage, and so on. "If I am perfect, no one can criticize me, no one can hurt me."

The aim of wanting to become "perfect" can work as a powerful force against an effective therapy. This is particularly true of narcissistic patients whose ego-ideal of perfection is linked with mechanisms of deep splitting, repression, and projection. Patients with the character disorder of excessive narcissism "seem to have such a need for personal admiration that they conceive of therapy as a means of making themselves more worthy of praise" (Wolberg, 1977, p. 880).

Wanting to become perfect is an egotistical preoccupation. By the same token, awareness and acceptance of one's darker side, with its destructive impulses and feelings of hatred, give one the freedom to choose. Striving for "wholeness" could be pinpointed in this context as the healthy aim contrasting with the sick and unrealistic aim of perfection. In this psychological sense the jargon term "wholeness" should mean healing the split between opposite feelings, tolerating, integrating the two sides of ambivalence, seeing realistically our shortcomings while trying to overcome them. In the struggle to restrain and harness our primitive impulses it is essential to distinguish between fantasy and reality. The more clearly we recognize the forbidden, repressed urges of sex, violence, and wanton cruelty in ourselves, the more our freedom increases. By becoming aware of our unconscious fantasies and knowing that we have not actually committed the fantasized crime that we kept hidden for so long, we free ourselves from guilt. By recognizing our destructive impulse as it stirs, we acquire the freedom of choice to translate it into reality there and then or to refrain from acting, or, preferably, to channel the same energy towards some constructive thought process and action.

Finally, it is essential to distinguish between neurotic perfectionism and striving to do one's best, while being guided by ideals. In psychoanalytic theory the concept of "perfection" is linked with the repression of its opposite— murky primitive forces. In Freud's explanation ". . . the 'urge towards perfection' of mankind is no other than an ever-repeated reaction against the primitive, amoral impulses which persist in the unconscious and are ever demanding satisfaction" (Ferenczi, 1926, p. 382). This is a one-sided, individualistic view. The instinctual roots of many ideals, such as altruism, respect, and care for others, self-restraint, self-sacrifice, lie in our nature as social "small group animals" (Molnos, 1979). If guided by social values and tempered by realism, a striving for perfection becomes a constructive driving force. This applies to both the patient and the therapist. Our wish to achieve the best possible outcome for our patients is not neurotic perfectionism. It springs from human concern for the other person and from professional dedication. In this case the striving for perfection is balanced by a realistic assessment of the patient's and our own resources.

## The question of aims: avoidance or terminological uncertainty

The question of the aim of psychotherapy is not often discussed in any depth. Looking across the range of treatment modalities from psychoanalysis through long- and medium-term psychotherapies towards brief dynamic psychotherapy, we find increasingly precise formulations of aims.

At one extreme of this continuum stands the very question of whether we need to formulate aims at all. There are many psychoanalysts and psychotherapists "who consider goals to be an extremely arbitrary matter". Some authors mention *goallessness* as "the procedural stance essential to technical analytic work" (Wolberg, 1977, p. 743).

At the other end of this spectrum, those practising forms of brief dynamic psychotherapy tend to be concerned with setting specific and explicit therapeutic aims to be attained at the end of the therapy.

There is terminological uncertainty too. Should we talk about therapeutic "aims" or "goals"? The latter have to do with consciously worked-out strategies and tactics, with planning, decision-making, and targeting. A "goal" is associated with commercial, marketing activities and competitive sports. Either the ball enters the net, or it does not. It can be observed and measured according to whether the set target has been hit or not. American authors (e.g. Saul, Wolberg) use "goal", while writers in this country (e.g. Balint, Fairbairn, Malan, Winnicott) favour the word "aim". Others replace "aim" with an even softer expression, such as the "concerns of psychotherapy" (Cohn, 1986, pp. 335–337).

We can settle for the term "aim", which indicates direction and, at the same time and in contrast to "goal", also allows for therapeutic shortcomings. As long as one is on the right track or course, one can *approximate* the aim, even if it might never be reached completely. In this sense "aim" is nearly synonymous with "ideal".

### Negative goals inherited from medicine or jargon

One way of avoiding the question, "What are the aims of psychotherapy?", is to formulate negative aims. "Lasting symptom relief", "freeing the patient from his neurosis", "preventing a neurosis from developing" belong to the category of negative aims and reflect the influence of medicine on the practice of psychotherapy. Nothing is said about what will replace the symptoms or the neurosis.

Probably Freud himself ". . . cared about a change of personality only in so far as it would guarantee a permanent cure of symptoms. Freud's goal is thus essentially to be defined in a negative manner: gaining 'freedom from'" (Horney, 1942, p. 21). Today the generally accepted formulation of the aim of all analytic psychotherapies—namely, to bring about fundamental changes in the individual— sounds positive. It actually only says that there will be profound as opposed to superficial changes. It does not say what changes we are aiming at.

Also those who favour a neat separation between therapeutic and religious aims without considering their closeness might assign to psychotherapy negative aims only: "The formal roles of psychotherapist and minister of religion are radically distinct. . . . The one aims at the healthy functioning of the psyche, the other at the spiritual well-being of the soul" (O'Doherty, 1974, pp. 213–214). One is left wondering how the "healthy functioning of the psyche" can be independent or separate from the "spiritual well-being of the soul" and vice versa . . .

Where we find positive aims for psychotherapy, there is often a tendency to present as complete an inventory of coveted achievements as possible rather than to strive for conceptual clarity (Cooper, 1974, p. 254).

Positive aims of psychotherapy are expressed through concepts like "personal growth", "individuation", "wholeness", "maturation", "self-realization", and so on. Unless accompanied by a clear definition, such words are either empty jargon or boast of grandiose ideas about therapeutic outcome. They are misleading general terms, open to widely differing definitions. They lure patient and therapist alike into following some unrealistic idea of perfection that might rob them of a rightful satisfaction with what already has been achieved.

## *The aims of the patient and third parties*

All those involved—the patient, the therapist, the patient's partner, relatives and friends, the therapist's supervisor— have tacit and often differing fantasies and expectations of what the outcome of the therapy ought to be. These expectations amount to unspoken aims that guide their thinking, actions, and attitudes towards the therapy and consequently influence it.

Unconscious non-therapeutic aims are part of the resistance of the unconscious against change. To help the patient to bring such unconscious aims to consciousness is the therapist's task.

There are aims in psychotherapy that the patient and the therapist naturally share. For instance, there is always an explicit, or tacit, agreement that the therapy should lead to eliminating the patient's presenting symptoms. However, patient and therapist might differ on the steps to be taken to get rid of those symptoms.

The patient's immediate aim might be unattainable because it is bound to an impossible condition: while he wants to get rid of his symptoms, he does not want to go through the pain that intrapsychic change entails. The therapist's aim is virtually the opposite. The disappearance of the symptom is not her first and immediate aim, because she knows that only intrapsychic change, which is of necessity painful, will produce the desired effect and eliminate the symptom.

The patient might not be clear about what he wants from psychotherapy, or his aims might be dictated by the very neurosis that his psychotherapy is expected to cure. His idea of the final aim, of what has to be achieved at the end of the therapy, does not necessarily coincide with that of the therapist. Moreover, there might be conflict with what others, such as the referring doctor or a particularly close friend or relative, have in mind.

Some patients seek psychotherapy in order consciously or unconsciously to influence or manipulate someone close to them. To a certain extent all patients come to therapy with a mixture of therapeutic and non-therapeutic or anti-therapeutic aims. The narcissistic person hopes to become more worthy of admiration as a result of therapy; the irate spouse wants the therapist to see how awful the other half is; the overweight patient wants advice on how to lose weight—which, if given, will not be followed; the guilty obsessive demands instant reassurance—which, if given, will not help; and so on. The therapist who, from the goodness of her heart or because of inexperience or her own guilt feelings, gives in to such pressures without challenging them, thus colluding with the person's neurotic, non-therapeutic aims, might soon find it difficult to shift the situation, and in the end she might be rejected by the patient.

## An attempt at formulating aims

If we do not spell out the unspoken aims of the therapy, at least for ourselves, they will remain hidden, exerting unrecognized influences. Setting merely negative aims is not the answer. At any rate, it would be a fruitless undertaking, an exercise in self-deception. "While the removal of symptoms is a worthwhile act, and is sometimes all the patient requests, the nature of psychologically derived symptoms is such that wider aims are nearly always implied" (Ryle, 1982, p. 3).

In order to attain some conceptual clarity about the aims of psychotherapy in general, or of a particular therapy, I suggest that we should make a *tripartite distinction between final, intermediate, and immediate aims,* even though they operate simultaneously most of the time. At the one end of this continuum, the ultimate aims of psychotherapy are indistinguishable from general human ideals embedded in the entire value system in which we live. At the other end, the immediate aims in the session coincide with the management of the patient and establishing the framework of the kind of psychotherapy we practice.

## Immediate aims
## and setting the therapeutic framework

Immediate aims in the here-and-now can be best shown in relation to the first session of a brief dynamic psychotherapy. These aims are to create and define the setting, the framework, to correct false expectations, as well as—and most importantly—to establish a good rapport and a therapeutic alliance.

One of the therapist's immediate aims is to find out whether there is third-party interference at the start of the therapy. Has the patient come of his own free will, or has he been pushed by someone close to him or even threatened with abandonment if he does not get himself into therapy?

Other subsidiary but interlinked and still immediate aims are to clarify and establish the parameters and boundaries of the relationship. This contract will vary greatly from one therapeutic school to another. In the pre-therapy interview, a psychoanalyst might explain to the patient that he would be expected to associate freely and lie on the couch. The brief dynamic psychotherapist might or might not explain to the patient who expects the couch why she does not use it and prefers to talk face to face. She would regard the first contact with the patient as the start of the therapy. From the very first moment she would use the time to monitor the patient's responses, in order to make sure that the patient has the psychic strength (or ego strength) to bear the unavoidable pain that is to come. Her immediate aim is to get as close to the patient as he can bear.

Explanations and clarifications lower the initial anxiety. Most counsellors and many psychotherapists do their best to put the patient at ease in the first session. Brief dynamic therapists' immediate aim is not to lower the initial anxiety, but to use it to help the patient to break through his defensive wall and to get to the core of the problem as fast as he can bear it. Therefore, anxiety-lowering explanations will be kept to a minimum. In the first session or "trial therapy" (Davanloo, 1980e, pp. 99–128; Molnos, 1986b), the therapist tests whether the patient has sufficient ego-strength to go beyond his habitual defences and to experience his true feelings to the full in the here-and-now. That test will decide whether or not the patient is suitable for this type of brief therapy. During the challenge of the defences, the resistance will increase and the therapeutic alliance will be in the balance. After the successful confrontation and the patient passing through his defensive barrier, the rapport and therapeutic alliance will become very strong. In all cases, the therapist will make sure that there is a good rapport at the end of the first session.

## Intermediate aims and therapeutic technique

Intermediate aims are those we pursue over many sessions and even throughout the duration of the therapy. They are inextricably linked with psychotherapeutic technique. With a silently choked patient, the intermediate aim might be to enable him to free himself from the inner blockage and experience the freedom of talking spontaneously. With a raging patient, the intermediate aim might be to put him in touch with his tender or sad feelings, with his pain, against which he is defending himself.

All along her work the brief therapist's intermediate aim is to apply the principles, techniques, and procedures of analytic psychotherapy in an active way and in the patient's best interest. Or we could say it in a more precise way: the therapist's intermediate aim at any one point in therapy is to follow and apply the basic analytic principles (chapter 2), thus facilitating corrective emotional experiences (Alexander & French, 1946, pp. 66–70), together with the correct cognitive recognition of internal and external reality as well as bringing about behavioural changes in his daily life.

Positive aims formulated by psychoanalysts tend to be intermediate aims, as they mostly describe the technique. "If our aim continues to be to verbalize the nascent conscious in terms of the transference, then we are practising analysis"

(Winnicott, 1965, pp. 169-170). The aims formulated by Freud—namely, "overcoming the patient's resistance" and "making the unconscious conscious"—are also intermediate aims.

The same formulations can be adapted to delineate intermediate aims in group-analytic psychotherapy. Paraphrasing Winnicott, we could say that one of the intermediate aims is to help the group to verbalize its nascent conscious in terms of the multiple transferences in the here-and-now. Or we could state that another intermediate aim is to help the group to overcome its resistance, or that the most important intermediate aim is to make the group unconscious conscious in the here-and-now.

## Final aims:
### their closeness to religious and cultural ideals

Ultimate or final aims are like ideals. They can never be reached completely, though they may be approximated at the end of a successful therapy or months, even years, afterwards.

To touch the question of ultimate or final aims means to open the Pandora's box of diverse cultural traditions and language. Such aims can only be formulated within a given metapsychological or philosophical view of the human being, of who we are and where we are going. Such a vision is deeply embedded in the particular culture and its religious values.

Therefore, together with other fundamental problems, the question of the ultimate aim of psychotherapy can only be answered within the total context of a particular cultural, religious, social, and political climate. The answer will depend on the particular metapsychology to which we cleave, which, in turn, will be influenced by how we view humankind's role on earth—that is, our *Weltanschauung*. The question, in fact, pertains to what the Germans call *Geistes-*

*wissenschaften*—"the sciences of the (human) spirit", for which we do not have a matching expression in English. The concept *Geist* in this sense remains untranslated in most languages, and "the Arts", the English equivalent of *Geistes-wissenschaften*, excludes the idea of "science" altogether.

For more than a century, psychology and later psychotherapy have struggled to distance themselves from philosophy and religion, to be counted amongst the natural sciences. In the process they have lost sight of the fact that we cannot deal with the psyche without having to sort out moral questions as well. At first it would seem that the etymology of the very term "psychotherapy", with its meaning of "caring for the soul", can be dismissed as a historical relic, without any significance for today's science or psychotherapy practice. But can it?

If the final aims of psychotherapy are left unspoken or are stated in negative formulations or are lost in a multitude of verbal expressions, it is partly because the coincidental nature of psychotherapeutic and moral aims is disturbing to scientific thinking.

As soon as we define psychotherapeutic aims in positive terms, of necessity we have to include imperatives for relationships with others. By doing so, we take sides on moral, ethical, and religious issues as well. We can no longer keep the aims of psychotherapy on safe neutral ground.

We hope that as a result of the therapy the patient will be a more contented person than he was at the start of it, at ease with himself and those close to him as well as others. If the person starts behaving destructively towards others, enjoys inflicting pain without remorse, acts hurtfully towards the weak and vulnerable or surreptitiously towards those in authority in order to have his own way at any cost, we will recoil from declaring that his therapy has been successful. Why so, if the ex-patient is happy with his new-found ruthlessness? Simply because we believe in a certain value system, because we find it impossible to accept that anyone can be truly content or happy in the long run by ignoring the values by which society exists.

The coincidental nature of psychotherapeutic final aims and religious and cultural ideals appears in many instances in the practice of psychotherapy.

In psychotherapy the patient has to reach the point where he can let go of the past and of those longings that life cannot fulfil and try to seek satisfaction in more realistic ways. ". . . the aim of therapy is not to make up to patients for the love they have missed, but to help them work through their feelings about not having it" (Malan, 1979, p. 141). As long as one is entangled in a running battle with one's past, with all the awful things that have happened, one cannot be entirely oneself. One is still in some way enmeshed with significant persons of the past, and dependent on them, directly or by opposition.

The acceptance of what happened in the past, experiencing the rage about it, yes, but then letting it go, whatever the deprivation, injustice and unfairness of it all, learning to live with one's guilt and pain are considerable positive achievements in any successful therapy.

When we help the patient to face reality, to accept and openly express his feelings about it in the session, we implicitly value truth and honesty more than deception and self-deception. When we help the patient to recognize the nature of his interactions with people from several angles, including the point of view of those who depend on him or oppose him, we value a sense of responsibility and sensitivity towards others more than self-centred blindness to them.

When we take measures to contain a patient who is in danger of seriously harming himself, we value health and life more than illness and death. We believe that life has a meaning.

When we resist colluding with a patient who wants us to enslave him, we not only obey the analytic rule of abstaining from fulfilling roles the patient tends to impose on us, but we also value freedom more than slavery in human relations, equality more than inequality. All these values that imbue most therapies coincide with prevalent religious and cultural ideals.

## A final aim for brief dynamic psychotherapy

Today it is a fundamental tenet of all analytically based psychotherapies that internal problems originate in relationships. They re-emerge in relationships. They also can be healed through relationships. The relationship with the therapist, or the multiple relationships in the analytic group, should offer the patient the "corrective emotional experience" (Alexander & French, 1946, pp. 60–70) that has this healing effect. It is also through the therapeutic relationship that the patient reaches a deeper understanding of the psychic mechanisms underlying his troubles.

Psychic "improvement" means an increased ability to be oneself, to fulfil one's essence, one's potential, while relating constructively to other human beings. Relating positively to others and developing, "improving" oneself, are inseparably linked.

No significant step in a process of "personal growth", "individuation", "self-realization", "maturation", "becoming whole", and so on can be achieved outside interpersonal relationships. Indeed, it would be difficult to conceive of a successful psychotherapy without significant improvements in the patient's relationships with others. The newly acquired ability to establish a close and lasting relationship with a suitable person is the best proof that a therapy has been successful.

*The final or central aim of psychotherapy is to enable the patient to feel entirely himself while being with others* and while he tolerates others to be themselves too. The tacit rules of such togetherness of distinct individuals will vary, along with the concepts of the "individual" and its associated degrees of tolerance, appreciation, respect, or disapproval in different cultures.

Psychoanalysis, psychoanalytically based long- and short-term individual psychotherapy, and group-analytic psychotherapy share the same ultimate objective—namely, to achieve fundamental changes in the individual. This fundamental change should consist in the person having "learnt" to be himself while being with others. In other words, the central, overriding, and ultimate aim of a complete psychodynamic therapy is both to find one's own unique individuality and to be able to hold on to it while relating to others in a mutually constructive, life-enhancing way. This is an ideal and, as such, can by definition never be reached completely. Successful therapy or not, none of us can relate to everyone. Therefore, in practice, this ideal central and ultimate aim has to be amplified: to learn to choose and select those people and situations in which mutually constructive relationships can flourish and to learn to modulate distances in relationships and settings that might potentially be destructive.

# REFERENCES AND BIBLIOGRAPHY

Aagaard, S. (1988). Time, youth and analytic group psycho-therapy. *Group Analysis, 21,* 4, 299–310.

Adler, G., & Myerson, P. G. (Eds.) (1973). *Confrontation in psychotherapy.* New York: Science House.

Alexander, F. (1950). *Psychosomatic medicine: its principles and applications.* New York: W. W. Norton.

Alexander, F. (1961). *The scope of psychoanalysis: selected papers of Franz Alexander, 1921–1961.* New York: Basic Books.

Alexander, F. (1980). The dynamics of psychotherapy in the light of learning theory. In: J. Marmor & S.M. Woods (Eds.), *The interface between the psychodynamic and behavioral therapies* (pp. 1–16). New York: Plenum Medical Book.

Alexander, F., & French, T. M. (1946). *Psychoanalytic therapy: principles and applications.* Lincoln, NE, & London: University of Nebraska Press, 1974.

Appelbaum, S. A. (1975). Parkinson's law in psychotherapy. *International Journal of Psychoanalytic Psychotherapy, 4,* 426–436.

Appelbaum, S. A. (1981). *Effecting change in psychotherapy.* New York: Jason Aronson.

Archer, D., & Gartner, R. (1984). *Violence and crime in cross-national perspective.* New Haven, CT: Yale University Press, 1987.

Ardrey, R. (1961). *African genesis: a personal investigation into the animal origins and nature of man.* London: Collins, 1971.

Ardrey, R. (1967). *The territorial imperative: a personal inquiry into the animal origins of property and nations.* London: Collins.

Arlow, J. A. (1984). Disturbances of the sense of time. *Psychoanalytic Quarterly, 53,* 13–37.

Balint, M. (1948). On genital love. In: M. Balint, *Primary love and psychoanalytic technique.* (pp. 109–120). London: Tavistock, 1965. [Reprinted London: Karnac Books, 1985.]

Balint, M. (1952). *Primary love and psychoanalytic technique.* London: Tavistock, 1965. [Reprinted London: Karnac Books, 1985.]

Balint, M. (1957). *The doctor, his patient, and the illness.* New York: International Universities Press.

Balint, M. (1968). *The basic fault: therapeutic aspects of regression.* London: Tavistock. [Reprinted London: Karnac Books, 1979.]

Balint, M., Ornstein, P. H., & Balint, E. (1972). *Focal psychotherapy, an example of applied psychoanalysis.* London: Tavistock.

Beck, M. (1979). Family members' perception and use of time: an element in family therapy. *Family Therapy, 1,* 5.

Behr, H., & Hearst, L. E. (guest Eds.) (1990). Special section: block training in group analysis. *Group Analysis, 23* (4), 339–375.

Bell, P. M. (1975). Sense of time. *New Scientist,* 15 May, p. 406.

Bergler, E., & Roheim, G. (1946). Psychology of time perception. *Psychoanalytic Quarterly, 26,* 190.

Bergson, H. (1889/1910). *Time and free will: an essay on the immediate data of consciousness.* London: Allen & Unwin.

Berkowitz, L. (1962). *Aggression: a social psychological analysis.* New York: McGraw-Hill.

Bertalanffy, L. von (1967). *Robots, men and minds: psychology in the modern world.* New York: George Braziller.

Bertalanffy, L. von (1968). *General system theory: foundations, development, applications*. London: Penguin, 1973.

Bettelheim, B. (1943). Individual and mass behaviour in extreme situations. *Journal of Abnormal Psychology, 38*, 417–452.

Bion, W. R. (1961). *Experiences in groups and other papers*. London: Tavistock, 1974.

Bion, W. R. (1970). *Attention and interpretation: a scientific approach to insight in psycho-analysis and groups*. London: Tavistock, 1975.

Bliss, E. L. (Ed.) (1962). *Roots of behaviour*. Riverside, NJ: Hafner, 1970.

Bloom, B. L. (1981). Focused single-session therapy: initial development and evaluation. In: S. H. Budman (Ed.), *Forms of brief therapy* (pp. 167–216). New York & London: Guilford Press.

Blumenberg, H. (1986). *Lebenszeit und Weltzeit*. Frankfurt: Surkamp.

Bolter, J. D. (1984). *Turing's man: Western culture in the computer age*. London: Duckworth.

Bonaparte, M. (1940). Time and the unconscious. *International Journal of Psychoanalysis, 21*, 427–468.

Boris, H. (1973). Confrontation in the analysis of the transference resistance. In: G. Adler & P. G. Myerson (Eds.), *Confrontation in psychotherapy* (pp. 181–206). New York: Science House.

Bowlby, J. (1953). *Child care and the growth of love*. London: Penguin Books, 1990.

Bowlby, J. (1969). *Attachment and loss. Vol. I, Attachment*. London: Penguin Books, 1978.

Bowlby, J. (1973). *Attachment and loss. Vol. II, Separation: anxiety and anger*. London: Penguin Books, 1978.

Bowlby, J. (1979). *The making & breaking of affectional bonds*. London: Tavistock/Routledge, 1992.

Bowlby, J. (1980). *Attachment and loss. Vol. III, Loss, sadness and depression*. London: The Hogarth Press and the Institute of Psycho-Analysis.

Bowlby, J. (1988). *A secure base: clinical applications of attachment theory*. London: Routledge.

Brandon, S. G. F. (1951). *Time and mankind.* London: Hutchinson.

Bräutigam, W., Knauss, W., & Wolff, H. H. (Eds.) (1983). *Erste Schritte in der Psychotherapy. Erfahrungen von Medizinstudenten, Patienten und Ärzten mit Psychotherapy—Michael Balint als Lehrer.* Berlin: Springer-Verlag.

Brizer, D. A., & Crowner, M. L. (Eds.) (1989). *Current approaches to the prediction of violence.* Washington, DC: American Psychiatric Press.

Brown, D. G. (1977). Drowsiness in the countertransference. *International Review of Psycho-Analysis, 4,* 481–492.

Brown, D., & Pedder, J. (1979). *Introduction to psychotherapy: an outline of psychodynamic principles and practice.* London: Tavistock Publications.

Budman, S. H. (Ed.) (1981a). *Forms of brief therapy.* New York: Guilford Press.

Budman, S. H. (1981b). Looking toward the future. In: S. H. Budman (Ed.), *Forms of brief therapy* (pp. 461–467). New York: Guilford Press.

Budman, S. H., & Gurman, A. S. (1988). *Theory and practice of brief therapy.* London: Hutchinson.

Budman, S. H., Hoyt, M. F., & Friedman, S. (Eds.) (1992). *The first session in brief therapy.* New York: Guilford Press.

Buie, D. H., Jr., & Adler, G. (1973). Uses of confrontation in the psychotherapy of borderline cases. In: G. Adler & P.G. Myerson (Eds.), *Confrontation in psychotherapy* (pp. 123–146). New York: Science House.

Burrow, T. (1927). *The social basis of consciousness.* New York: Harcourt Brace.

Burrow, T. (1937). *The biology of human conflict.* New York: Macmillan.

Burrow, T. (1949). *Neurosis of man.* London: Routledge & Kegan Paul.

Butcher, J. N., & Koss, M. P. (1978). Research on brief and crisis-oriented therapies. In: S. L. Garfield & A. E. Bergin (Eds.), *Handbook of psychotherapy and behavior change.* New York: John Wiley & Sons.

Calabresi, R., & Cohen, J. (1968). Personality and time attitudes. *Journal of Abnormal Psychology, 73,* 431.

Campbell, J. (Ed.) (1957). *Man and time: papers from the*

*Eranos Yearbooks*. Princeton, NJ: Princeton University Press, 1983.

Carthy, J. D., & Ebling, F. J., Jr. (Eds.) (1964). *The natural history of aggression*. New York & London: Academic Press.

Castelnuovo-Tedesco, P. (1965). *The twenty-minute hour: a guide to brief psychotherapy for the physician*. Washington, DC: American Psychiatric Press.

Chasseguet-Smirgel, J. (1986). *Sexuality and mind: the role of the father and the mother in the psyche*. New York & London: New York University Press.

Ciompi, L. (1988). *Aussenwelt-Innenwelt: die Entstehung von Zeit, Raum und psychischen Strukturen*. Göttingen: Vandenhoeck & Ruprecht.

Cloudsley-Thompson, J. L. (1980). *Biological clocks: their function in nature*. London: Weidenfeld & Nicholson.

Cohn, F. S. (1957). Time and the ego. *Psychoanalytic Quarterly, 26*, 168.

Cohn, H. W. (1986). The double context: on combining individual and group therapy. *Group Analysis, 19* (4), 327–339.

Cohn, H. W. (1988). Phenomenological elements in group therapy: papers from continental Europe. *Group Analysis, 21* (4), 283–287.

Conder, P. J. (1949). Individual distance. *Ibis, 91*, 649–655.

Console, W. A., Simons, R. C., & Rubinstein, M. (1977). *The first encounter: the beginnings in psychotherapy*. New York: Jason Aronson.

Cooper, C. (1974). Short-term therapy. In: V. Varma (Ed.), *Psychotherapy today* (pp. 250–264). London: Constable.

Darwin, Ch. (1871). *Descent of man*. London: John Murray.

Davanloo, H. (Ed.) (1978a). *Basic principles and techniques in short-term dynamic psychotherapy*. New York: Spectrum.

Davanloo, H. (1978b). Basic methodology and technique of short-term dynamic psychotherapy. "The case of the cement-mixer man." In: H. Davanloo (Ed.), *Basic principles* (pp. 343–388). New York: Spectrum.

Davanloo, H. (1978c). Continuum of psychotherapeutic possibilities and basic psychotherapeutic techniques. In: H. Davanloo (Ed.), *Basic principles* (pp. 74–81). New York: Spectrum.

Davanloo, H. (1978d). Evaluation, criteria for selection of patients for short-term dynamic psychotherapy: a meta-psychological approach. In: H. Davanloo (Ed.), *Basic principles* (pp. 9–34). New York: Spectrum.

Davanloo, H. (1978e). Short-term dynamic psychotherapy of one to two sessions' duration. "The case of the woman with the fear of losing her husband." In: H. Davanloo (Ed.), *Basic principles* (pp. 307–326). New York: Spectrum.

Davanloo, H. (1978f). Techniques of short-term dynamic psychotherapy. "The case of the man obsessed with the small size of his genitals." In: H. Davanloo (Ed.), *Basic principles* (pp. 469–489). New York: Spectrum.

Davanloo, H. (1978g). "The case of the angry, childlike woman." In: H. Davanloo (Ed.), *Basic principles* (pp. 247–266). New York: Spectrum.

Davanloo, H. (1978h). "The case of the teeth-grinding woman." In: H. Davanloo (Ed.), *Basic principles* (pp. 171–199). New York: Spectrum.

Davanloo, H. (Ed.) (1980a). *Short-term dynamic psychotherapy.* New York: Jason Aronson.

Davanloo, H. (1980b). A method of short-term dynamic psychotherapy. In: H. Davanloo (Ed.), *Short-term dynamic psychotherapy* (pp. 43–71). New York: Jason Aronson.

Davanloo, H. (1980c). Response to interpretation. In: H. Davanloo (Ed.), *Short-term dynamic psychotherapy* (pp. 75–91). New York: Jason Aronson.

Davanloo, H. (1980d). The technique of crisis evaluation and intervention. In: H. Davanloo (Ed.), *Short-term dynamic psychotherapy* (pp. 245–281). New York: Jason Aronson.

Davanloo, H. (1980e). Trial therapy. In: H. Davanloo (Ed.), *Short-term dynamic psychotherapy* (pp. 98–128). New York: Jason Aronson.

Davanloo, H. (1986). Intensive short-term psychotherapy with highly resistant patients. *International Journal of Short-Term Psychotherapy, 1* (2), 107–133, 239–255.

Davanloo, H. (1990). *Unlocking the unconscious: selected papers of H. Davanloo, MD.* Chichester: John Wiley.

Davanloo, H., & Sifneos, P. E. (1980). The technique of crisis support. In: H. Davanloo (Ed.), *Short-term dynamic psychotherapy* (pp. 283–302). New York: Jason Aronson.

Davanloo, H., & Yung C. (1978). Where does evaluation end and therapy begin? In: H. Davanloo (Ed.), *Basic principles* (pp. 291–306). New York: Spectrum.

Dawkins, R. (1976). *The selfish gene.* Oxford: Oxford University Press.

Dollard, J., Doob, L. W., Miller, N. E., Mowrer, O. H., & Sears, R. R. (1939). *Frustration and aggression.* Westport, CT: Greenwood Press, 1990.

Doob, L. W. (1971). *Patterning of time.* New Haven, CT: Yale University Press.

Drisko, J. W. (1978). Time-limited therapy with children: the impact of emotional disturbance on time understanding. *Smith College Studies in Social Work, 48,* 107.

DuBois, F. S. (1954). The sense of time and its relation to psychiatric illness. *American Journal of Psychiatry, 111,* 46.

Edelstein, M. G. (1990). *Symptom analysis: a method of brief therapy.* New York: W. W. Norton.

Eibl-Eibesfeldt, I. (1961). Fighting behavior in animals. *Scientific American,* December.

Eisenstein, S. (1980). The contributions of Franz Alexander. In: H. Davanloo (Ed.), *Short-term dynamic psychotherapy* (pp. 25–41). New York: Jason Aronson.

Eliade, M. (1954). *The myth of the eternal return, or cosmos and history.* Princeton, NJ: Princeton University Press.

Elias, N. (1937/1939). *Über den Prozess der Zivilisation.* Prague: Academia Verlag (Vol. I). Basel: Verlag Haus zum Falken (Vol. II).

Elias, N. (1984). *Über die Zeit.* Frankfurt am Main: Suhrkamp.

Erickson, M. H., Rossi, E. L., & Rossi, S. I. (1976). *Hypnotic realities: the induction of clinical hypnosis and forms of indirect suggestion.* New York: Irvington Publishers.

Erikson, E. H. (1950). *Childhood and society.* New York: W. W. Norton.

Erikson, E. H. (1980). Elements of a psychoanalytic theory of psychosocial development. In: S. I. Greenspan & G. H. Pollock (Eds.), *The course of life, Vol. I* (pp. 11–61). East Adelphi, MD: Mental Health Study Center, NIMH.

Fairbairn, W. R. D. (1952). *Psychoanalytic studies of the personality.* London: Routledge & Kegan Paul, 1978.

Ferenczi, S. (1926). *Further contributions to the theory and tech-*

*nique of psycho-analysis.* London: Hogarth Press, 1955. [Reprinted London: Karnac Books, 1980.]

Ferenczi, S. (1945). Freud's influence on medicine. In: S. Lorand (Ed.), *Psychoanalysis today* (pp. 1–11). New York: International Universities Press.

Ferenczi, S. (1952). *First contributions to psycho-analysis.* London: Hogarth Press, 1955. [Reprinted London: Karnac Books, 1980.]

Ferenczi, S. (1955). *Final contributions to the problems and methods of psycho-analysis.* London: Hogarth Press. [Reprinted London: Karnac Books, 1980.]

Ferenczi, S., & Rank, O. (1925). *The Development of Psychoanalysis.* New York: Nervous & Mental Diseases Publishing. [Reprinted London: Karnac Books, 1986.]

Fisch, R., Weakland, J. H., & Segal, L. (1982). *The tactics of change: doing therapy briefly.* San Francisco, CA: Jossey-Bass, 1983.

Fisher, S., & Fisher, R. L. (1953). Unconscious conceptions of parental figures as a factor influencing perception of time. *Journal of Personality, 21,* 496.

Flegenheimer, W. V. (1982). *Techniques of brief psychotherapy.* New York: Jason Aronson.

Fletcher, R. (1957). *Instinct in man.* London: Allen & Unwin, 1988.

Flood, R., & Lockwood, M. (Eds.) (1986). *The nature of time.* Oxford: Blackwell.

Forrester, J. (1990). Dead on time: Lacan's theory of temporality. In: J. Forrester (Ed.), *The seductions of psychoanalysis, Freud, Lacan and Derrida* (pp. 168–218). Cambridge: Cambridge University Press.

Forrester, J. (1992). "In the beginning was repetition": on inversions and reversals in psychoanalytic time. *Time & Society, 1* (2), 287–300.

Foulkes, S. H. (1948). *Introduction to group-analytic psychotherapy: studies in the social integration of individuals and groups.* London: Maresfield Reprints, 1984.

Foulkes, S. H. (1964). *Therapeutic group analysis.* London: Allen & Unwin.

Foulkes, S. H. (1975). *Group-analytic psychotherapy: method and principles.* London: Gordon & Breach.

Foulkes, S. H. (1990a). *Group-analytic psychotherapy.* Three audio-tapes dictated by the author and text. I. History & basic principles. II. Therapeutic processes. III. The group conductor.) London: The Joint Publications Committee of The Institute of Group Analysis and The Group-Analytic Society (London).

Foulkes, S. H. (1990b). *Selected papers: psychoanalysis and group analysis.* London: Karnac Books.

Foulkes, S. H., & Anthony, E. J. (1957). *Group psychotherapy: the psychoanalytic approach.* London: Karnac Books, 1984.

Frankel, F. H. (1981). Short-term psychotherapy and hypnosis. *Psychotherapy and Psychosomatics, 35,* 236–243.

Fraser, J. T. (Ed.) (1966). *The voices of time.* Amherst, MA: University of Massachusetts Press, 1981.

Fraser, J. T. (1975). *Of time, passion, and knowledge.* Princeton, NJ: Princeton University Press, 1990.

Fraser, J. T. (Ed.) (1978a). *The study of time.* New York: Springer Verlag.

Fraser, J. T. (1978b). *Time as conflict.* Basel & Boston: Birkhäuser Verlag.

Fraser, J. T. (1981). Temporal levels and reality testing. *International Journal of Psychoanalysis, 62,* 3–26.

Fraser, J. T. (1982). *The genesis and evolution of time.* Amherst, MA: University of Massachusetts Press.

Fraser, J. T. (1987). *Time, the familiar stranger.* La Vergne: Tempus, 1989.

Fraser, J. T. (1992). Human temporality in a nowless universe. *Time & Society, 1* (2), 159–173.

Freud, S. (1895d). On the psychical mechanism of hysterical phenomena: preliminary communication. *Standard Edition, 2,* 3.

Freud, S. (1905e [1901]). Fragment of an analysis of a case of hysteria. *Standard Edition, 7,* 3.

Freud, S. (1909b). Analysis of a phobia in a five-year-old boy. *Standard Edition, 10,* 3.

Freud, S. (1909d). Notes upon a case of obsessional neurosis. *Standard Edition, 10,* 155.

Freud, S. (1911c [1910]). Psycho-analytic notes on an autobiographical account of a case of paranoia. *Standard Edition, 12,* 3.

# 102 REFERENCES AND BIBLIOGRAPHY

Freud, S. (1915e). The unconscious. *Standard Edition, 14*, 161.

Freud, S. (1918b [1914]). From the history of an infantile neurosis. *Standard Edition, 17*, 3.

Freud, S. (1920a). The psychogenesis of a case of female homosexuality. *Standard Edition, 18*, 147.

Friedman, H. (1973). Confrontation in the psychotherapy of adolescent patients. In: G. Adler & P. G. Myerson (Eds.), *Confrontation in psychotherapy* (pp. 347–367). New York: Science House.

Friedman, W. J. (1990). *About time.* Cambridge, MA: MIT Press.

Fromm, E. (1951). *The forgotten language.* New York: Rinehart.

Fromm, E. (1973). *The anatomy of human destructiveness.* Harmondsworth, Middlesex: Penguin Books, 1990.

Fubini, F. (1988). Work of time and work of clocks: the experience of the uncontainable and the emergence of the container. *Group Analysis, 21* (4), 311–323.

Garland, C. (1982). Taking the non-problem seriously. *Group Analysis, 15* (1), 4–14.

Gedo, J. E. (1984). *Psychoanalysis and its discontents.* New York: Guilford Press.

Gehlen, A. (1940). *Der Mensch, seine Natur und seine Stellung in der Welt.* Berlin: Junker und Dürrhaupt.

Gilliéron, E. (1981). Psychoanalysis and brief psychotherapy: some new considerations on the psychotherapeutic process. *Psychotherapy and Psychosomatics, 35*, 244–256.

Gilliéron, E. (1983). *Les psychothérapies brèves.* Paris: Presses Universitaires de France.

Glasser, R. (1972). *Time in French life and thought.* Manchester: Manchester University Press.

Golden, C. (1978). Implications of the interviewer's technique on selection criteria. "The case of the submissive woman." "The case of the man with a headache." In: H. Davanloo (Ed.), *Basic principles* (pp. 269–290). New York: Spectrum.

Gould, S. J. (1988). *Time's arrow—time's cycle: myth and methaphor in the discovery of geological time.* London: Penguin Books.

Graham, F. W. (1984). Why do people stop conducting groups? *Group Analysis, 17* (2), 166.

Grand, S., Rechetnick, J., Podrug, D., & Schwager, E. (1985). *Transference in brief psychotherapy: an approach to the study of psychoanalytic process.* Hillsdale, NJ: Analytic Press.

Greenson, R. (1967). *The technique and practice of psychoanalysis, Vol. I.* London: Hogarth Press and the Institute of Psycho-Analysis, 1978.

Groebel, J., & Hinde, R. A. (Eds.) (1989). *Aggression and war.* Cambridge: Cambridge University Press.

Grotjahn, M. (1983). Why do people stop conducting groups? *Group Analysis, 16* (3), 258.

Grotjahn, M. (1988). Being bored in group therapy. *Group Analysis, 21* (4), 361–362.

Gunn, J. (1973). *Violence in human society.* Newton Abbot: David & Charles.

Gurr, T. R., & Graham, H. D. (1969). *The history of violence in America.* New York: Bantam Books.

Gustafson, J. P. (1981). The complex secret of brief psychotherapy in the works of Malan and Balint. In: S. H. Budman (Ed.), *Forms of brief therapy* (pp. 83–128). New York & London: Guilford Press.

Gustafson, J. P. (1986). *The complex secret of brief psychotherapy.* New York: W. W. Norton.

Hall, E. T. (1959). *The silent language.* Greenwich, CT: Fawcett Publications.

Hall, E. T. (1983). *The dance of life: the other dimension of time.* New York: Anchor/Doubleday.

Hartocollis, P. (1986). *Time and timelessness or the varieties of temporal experience (A psychoanalytic inquiry).* Madison, CT: International Universities Press.

Hawking, S. (1988). *A brief history of time: from the big bang to black holes.* London: Bantam Press.

Haynal, A. (1988). *The technique at issue: controversies in psychoanalysis from Freud and Ferenczi to Michael Balint.* London: Karnac Books.

Hediger, H. (1955). *Studies of the psychology and behaviour of captive animals in zoos and circuses.* London: Butterworths.

Hernadi, P. (1992). Objective, subjective, intersubjective times. Guest editor's introduction. *Time & Society, 1* (2), 147–158.

Hill, C. E. (1989). *Therapist techniques and client outcomes: eight cases of brief psychotherapy.* London: Sage Publications.

Hinde, R. A. (1974). *Biological bases of human social behaviour*. New York: McGraw-Hill.

Høglend, P. (1993). Suitability for brief dynamic psychotherapy: psychodynamic variables as predictors of outcome. *Acta Psychiatrica Scandinavica, 88*, 104–110.

Høglend, P., Sørlie, T., Sørbye, O., Heyerdahl, O., & Amlo, S. (1992). Long-term changes after brief dynamic psychotherapy: symptomatic versus dynamic assessments. *Acta Psychiatrica Scandinavica, 86*, 165–172.

Holmes, J. (Ed.). (1991). *Textbook of psychotherapy in psychiatric practice*. Edinburgh & London: Churchill Livingstone.

Horney, K. (1939). *New ways in psychoanalysis*. New York: W. W. Norton.

Horney, K. (1942). *Self-analysis*. London: Routledge & Kegan Paul, 1962.

Horowitz, M. J. (1979). *States of mind*. New York: Plenum.

Horowitz, M. J. (1983). *Image formation and psychotherapy*. New York: Aronson.

Horowitz, M. J. (1986). *Stress response syndromes*. New York: Jason Aronson.

Horowitz, M. J., Marmar, C., Weiss, D. S., et al. (1984). Brief therapy for bereavement reactions. *Archives of General Psychiatry, 41*, 438–448.

Horowitz, M. J., Marmar, Ch., Krupnick, J., Wilner, N., Kaltreider, N., & Wallerstein, R. (1984). *Personality styles and brief psychotherapy*. New York: Basic Books.

Hoyt, M. F., Rosenbaum, R., & Talmon, M. (1992). Planned single-session psychotherapy. In: S. H. Budman, M. F. Hoyt, & S. Friedman (Eds.), *The first session in brief therapy* (pp. 59–86). New York: Guilford Press.

Husby, R. (1985). Short-term dynamic psychotherapy. III. A five-year follow-up of 36 neurotic patients. *Psychotherapy and Psychosomatics, 43*, 17–22.

Huxley, J. S. (1942). *Evolution: the modern synthesis*. London: Allen & Unwin.

Huxley, T. H., & Huxley, J. S. (1947). *Evolution and ethics, 1893–1943*. Millwood, NY: Kraus, 1972.

Johnson, D. H., & Gelso, C. J. (1980). The effectiveness of time limits in counseling and psychotherapy: a critical review. *The Counseling Psychologist, 9*, 70–83.

Jung, C. G. (1954). *The practice of psychotherapy: essays on the psychology of the transference and other subjects.* London: Routledge & Kegan, 1981.

Kaltreider, N., DeWitt, K., Weiss, D. S., & Horowitz, M. J. (1981). Patterns of individual change scales. *Archives of General Psychiatry, 38,* 1263–1269.

Kern, S. (1983). *The culture of time and space: 1880–1918.* London: Weidenfeld & Nicholson.

Klein, M. (1955). On identification. In: *Envy and gratitude and other works, 1946–1963.* London: Hogarth Press, 1980. [Reprinted London: Karnac Books, 1993.]

Kluft, R. P. (Ed.) (1990). *Incest-related syndromes of adult psychopathology.* Washington, DC: American Psychiatric Press.

Kortlandt, A. (1955). *Aspects and prospects of the concept of instinct.* Leyden: E. J. Brill.

Kubler, G. (1962). *The shape of time: remarks on the history of things.* New Haven, CT: Yale University Press.

Landes, D.S. (1983). *Revolution in time.* Cambridge, MA: Harvard University Press.

Laplanche, J., & Pontalis, J.-B. (1973). *The language of psychoanalysis.* London: Hogarth Press.

Leibovich, M. A. (1983). Why short-term psychotherapy for borderlines? *Psychotherapy and Psychosomatics, 39,* 1–9.

Leuzinger-Bohleber, M. (Ed.) (1985). *Psychoanalytische Kurztherapien. Zur Psychoanalyse in Institutionen.* Opladen: Westdeutscher Verlag.

Levin, S. (1973). Confrontation as a demand for change. In: G. Adler & P. G. Myerson (Eds.), *Confrontation in psychotherapy* (pp. 303–317). New York: Science House.

Lewin, K. (1936). *Resolving social conflicts.* Auburn: Condor Books, 1973.

Lindemann, E. (1944). Symptomatology and management of acute grief. *American Journal of Psychiatry, 101,* 141–148.

Lindemann, E. (1979). *Beyond grief: studies in crisis intervention.* New York: Jason Aronson.

Lorenz, K. (1952). *King Solomon's ring: new light on animal ways.* London: Methuen, 1970.

Lorenz, K. (1963). *On aggression.* London: Methuen, 1979.

Lorenz, K. (1977). *Behind the mirror: a search for a natural history of human knowledge.* London: Methuen.

McCallum, M. & Piper, W. E. (1990). A controlled study of effectiveness and patient suitability for short-term group psychotherapy. *International Journal of Group Psychotherapy, 40,* 431–452.

Macey, S. L. (1991). *Time: a bibliographic guide.* New York: Garland.

McGlashan, T. H., & Miller, G. H. (1982). The goals of psychoanalysis and psychoanalytic therapy. *Archives of General Psychiatry, 39,* 377–388.

McGrath, J. E., & Kelly, J.R. (1986). *Time and human interaction: toward a social psychology of time.* New York: Guilford Press.

McGrath, J. E. (Ed.) (1988). *The social psychology of time: new perspectives.* London: Sage.

Mahler, M., Pine, F., & Bergman, A. (1975). *The psychological birth of the human infant.* New York: Basic Books.

Malan, D. H. (1963). *A study of brief psychotherapy.* New York: Plenum, 1975.

Malan, D. H. (1976a). *The frontier of brief psychotherapy: an example of the convergence of research and clinical practice.* New York: Plenum.

Malan, D. H. (1976b). *Toward the validation of dynamic psychotherapy: a replication.* New York: Plenum.

Malan, D. H. (1978a). Evaluation criteria for selection of patients. In: H. Davanloo (Ed.), *Basic principles* (pp. 85–97). New York: Spectrum.

Malan, D. H. (1978b). Exploring the limits of brief psychotherapy. In: H. Davanloo (Ed.), *Basic principles* (pp. 43–67). New York: Spectrum.

Malan, D. H. (1978c). Principles of technique in short-term dynamic psychotherapy. In: H. Davanloo (Ed.), *Basic principles* (pp. 332–342). New York: Spectrum.

Malan, D. H. (1978d). Techniques of short-term dynamic psychotherapy. "The case of the woman in mourning." In: H. Davanloo (Ed.), *Basic principles* (pp. 455–468). New York: Spectrum.

Malan, D. H. (1979). *Individual psychotherapy and the science of psychodynamics.* London: Butterworth.

Malan, D. H. (1980a). Basic principles and technique of

the follow-up interview. In: H. Davanloo (Ed.), *Short-term dynamic psychotherapy* (pp. 349–377). New York: Jason Aronson.

Malan, D. H. (1980b). Criteria for selection. In: H. Davanloo (Ed.), *Short-term dynamic psychotherapy* (pp. 169–189). New York: Jason Aronson.

Malan, D. H. (1980c). The most important development since the discovery of the unconscious. In: H. Davanloo (Ed.), *Short-term dynamic psychotherapy* (pp. 13–23). New York: Jason Aronson.

Malan, D. H. (1980d). The nature of science and the validity of psychotherapy. In: H. Davanloo (Ed.), *Short-term dynamic psychotherapy* (pp. 319–347). New York: Jason Aronson.

Malan, D. H. (1986). Beyond interpretation: initial evaluation and technique in short-term dynamic psychotherapy. *International Journal of Short-Term Psychotherapy, 1* (2), 59–82 (Part I); 83–106 (Part II).

Malan, D. H., & Osimo, F. (1992). *Psychodynamics, training, and outcome in brief psychotherapy.* Oxford: Butterworth–Heinemann.

Mandel, H. P. (1981). *Short-term psychotherapy and brief treatment techniques: an annotated bibliography, 1920–1980.* New York: Plenum.

Mann, J. (1973a). Confrontation as a mode of teaching. In: G. Adler & P. G. Myerson (Eds.), *Confrontation in psychotherapy* (pp. 39–48). New York: Science House.

Mann, J. (1973b). *Time-limited psychotherapy.* Cambridge, MA: Harvard University Press, 1979.

Mann, J. (1981). The core of time-limited psychotherapy: time and the central issue. In: S. H. Budman (Ed.), *Forms of brief therapy* (pp. 25–43). New York: Guilford Press.

Mann, J., & Goldman, R. (1982). *A casebook in time-limited psychotherapy.* New York: McGraw-Hill.

Marmor, J. (1978). Current trends in psychotherapy. In: H. Davanloo (Ed.), *Basic principles* (pp. 1–7). New York: Spectrum.

Marmor, J. (1980a). Crisis intervention and short-term dynamic psychotherapy. In: H. Davanloo (Ed.), *Short-term dynamic psychotherapy* (pp. 237–243). New York: Aronson.

Marmor, J. (1980b). Dynamic psychotherapy and behavior therapy: are they irreconcilable? In: J. Marmor & S. M. Woods (Eds.), *The interface* (pp. 17–32). New York: Plenum.

Marmor, J. (1980c). Historical roots. In: H. Davanloo (Ed.), *Short-term dynamic psychotherapy* (pp. 3–12). New York: Jason Aronson.

Marmor, K. (1980d). The persistently suicidal risk. In: H. Davanloo (Ed.), *Short-term dynamic psychotherapy* (pp. 303–315). New York: Jason Aronson.

Marmor, J., & Woods, S. M. (Eds.) (1980). *The interface between the psychodynamic and behavioral therapies.* New York: Plenum.

Marziali, E. A. (1984). Prediction of outcome of brief psychotherapy from therapist interpretive interventions. *Archives of General Psychiatry, 41* (March), 301–305.

Marziali, E. A., & J. M. Sullivan (1980). Methodological issues in the content analysis of brief psychotherapy. *British Journal of Medical Psychology, 53,* 19–27.

Meerloo, J. (1950). Father time. *Psychiatric Quarterly, 24,* 657.

Meyerhoff, H. (1955). *Time in literature.* Berkeley & Los Angeles: University of California Press.

Miller, A. (1983). *For your own good: hidden cruelty in child rearing and the roots of violence.* London: Virago.

Molnos, A. (1979). The self-healing small group. *Group Analysis, 12* (3), 192–195.

Molnos, A. (1980). Healing "hidden dependence" through holding in the group. *Group Analysis, 13* (3), 183–191.

Molnos, A. (1984). The two triangles are four: a diagram to teach the process of dynamic brief psychotherapy. *British Journal of Psychotherapy, 1* (2), 112–125.

Molnos, A. (1986a). Selling dynamic brief psychotherapy and teaching the patient: reflections on a symposium. *British Journal of Psychotherapy, 2* (3), 201–207.

Molnos, A. (1986b). The process of short-term dynamic psychotherapy and the four triangles. *International Journal of Short-Term Psychotherapy, 1* (3), 161–177.

Molnos, A. (1986c). Anger that destroys and anger that heals: handling hostility in group analysis and in dynamic brief psychotherapy. *Group Analysis, 19,* 207–221.

# REFERENCES AND BIBLIOGRAPHY 109

Molnos, A. (1986d). The handling of the here-and-now in short-term dynamic psychotherapy. Paper presented to the *First European Symposium on Short-Term Psychotherapy*, Copenhagen, 7–11 July.

Molnos, A. (1986e). Role-playing the first session: a learning technique for short-term dynamic psychotherapy. Paper presented to the *First European Symposium on Short-Term Dynamic Psychotherapy*, Copenhagen, 7–11 July.

Molnos, A. (1986f). From video-recordings towards integrated thinking in brief psychotherapy: reflections after the First European Symposium on Short-Term Dynamic Psychotherapy, Copenhagen, 7–11 July 1986. *British Journal of Psychotherapy*, 3 (2), 165–171.

Molnos, A. (1990). *Our responses to a deadly virus: the group-analytic approach.* London: Karnac Books for the Group-Analytic Society (London) and the Institute of Group Analysis.

Molnos, A. (1991). Destructive idealization: a threat to our times. *Group Analysis*, 24, 133–145.

Molnos, A. (1992). *Waiting on wonder: verses of a lifetime from three continents in English and Hungarian.* London: Circle Press.

Money-Kyrle, R. (1971). The aim of psychoanalysis. *International Journal of Psycho-Analysis*, 52, 103–106.

Montagu A. (1976). *The nature of human aggression.* Oxford: Oxford University Press, 1987.

Montagu, M. F. A. (1956). *The biosocial nature of man.* Westport, CT: Greenwood Press, 1990.

Montagu, M. F. A. (1962). *Culture and the evolution of man.* New York: Oxford University Press.

Moore-Ede, M. C., Sulzman, F. R., & Fuller, C. A. (1982). *The clocks that time us.* Cambridge, MA: Harvard University Press.

Morris, R. (1984). *Time's arrow.* New York: Simon & Schuster.

Münz-Herzog, V. (1990). Block training in Zurich: the phenomenon of "time and rhythm". *Group Analysis*, 23 (4), 353–359.

Murray, J. (1973). The purpose of confrontation. In: G. Adler & P. G. Myerson (Eds.), *Confrontation in psychotherapy* (pp. 49–65). New York: Science House.

Musatti, C. L. (1950). *Trattato di psicoanalisi* (2 vols.). Turin: Giulio Einaudi Editore.

Myerson, P. G. (1973). The meanings of confrontation. In: G. Adler & P. G. Myerson (Eds.), *Confrontation in psychotherapy* (pp. 21–37). New York: Science House.

Needham, J. (1965). *Time and Eastern man.* (Henry Myers Lecture.) London: Royal Anthropological Institute. Occasional Paper No. 21.

Neuman, G. (Ed.) (1987). *Origins of human aggression.* New York: Human Science Press.

Newton-Smith, W. H. (1980). *The structure of time.* London: Routledge & Kegan Paul.

Nilsson, M. P. (1920). *Primitive time-reckoning.* Lund: C. W. K. Gleerup.

Nisbet, R. (1980). *History of the idea of progress.* New Brunswick, NJ: Transaction, 1994.

Noel, K. F., Green, B. L., Grace, M. C., et al. (1985). Empathy and outcome in brief focal dynamic therapy. *American Journal of Psychiatry, 142,* 917–921.

O'Doherty, E. (1974). *Religious therapy.* In: V. Varma (Ed.), *Psychotherapy today* (pp. 201–214). London: Constable.

O'Hanlon, W. H., & Weiner-Davis, M. (1989). *In search of solutions: a new direction in psychotherapy.* New York: W. W. Norton.

Olivieri-Larsson, R. (1991). "Block training in group analysis", *Group Analysis,* Special Section, *23* (4): 339–666. *Group Analysis, 24* (3), 335–337.

Orgler, H. (1974). Adlerian therapy. In: V. Varma (Ed.), *Psychotherapy today* (pp. 157–171). London: Constable.

Ornstein, R. E. (1969). *On the experience of time.* New Brunswick, NJ: Transaction, 1994.

Palmer, J. D. (1976). *An introduction to biological rhythms.* London: Academic Press.

Pardes, H., & Pincus, H. A. (1981). Brief therapy in the context of national mental health issues. In: S. H. Budman (Ed.), *Forms of brief therapy* (pp. 7–22). New York: Guilford Press.

Parker, T., & Allerton R. (1962). *The courage of his convictions.* London: Hutchinson.

Parkes, C. M., & Stevenson-Hinde, J. (Eds.) (1982). *The place of attachment in human behaviour.* London: Tavistock.

Peake, T. H., Borduin, Ch. M., & Archer, R. P. (1988). *Brief psychotherapies: changing frames of mind.* London: Sage.

Perls, F. S., Hefferline, R. F., & Goodman, P. (1951). *Gestalt therapy: excitement and growth in the human personality.* New York: Dell.

Pflüger, P.-M. (Ed.) (1984). *Trennung und Abschied—Chance zu neuem Leben.* Fellbach-Oeffingen: Verlag Adolf Bonz.

Piaget, J. (1969). *The child's conception of time.* London: Routledge & Kegan Paul.

Piper, W. E., Azim, H. F., Joyce, A. S., & McCallum, M. (1991). Transference interpretations, therapeutic alliance, and outcome in short-term individual psychotherapy. *Archives of General Psychiatry, 48* (10), 946–953.

Piper, W. E., Debbane, E. G., Bienvenu, J. P., de Carufel, F., & Garant, J. (1986). Relationships between the object focus of therapist interpretations and outcome in short-term individual psychotherapy. *British Journal of Medical Psychology, 59* (1), 1–11.

Piper, W. E., de Carufel, E. L., & Szkrumelak, N. (1985). Patient predictors of process and outcome in short-term individual psychotherapy. *Journal of Nervous and Mental Diseases, 173,* 726–733.

Piper, W. E., Hassan, F. A., McCallum, M, & Joyce, A. S. (1990). Patient suitability and outcome in short-term individual psychotherapy. *Journal of Consultinq and Clinical Psychology, 58,* 1–7.

Piper, W. E., McCallum M., & Azim, H. F. A. (1992). *Adaptation to loss through short-term group psychotherapy.* New York: Guilford Press.

Porter, R. (Ed.) (1968). *The role of learning in psychotherapy.* London: J. & A. Churchill.

Poulet, G. (1959). *Studies in human time.* Westport, CT: Greenwood Press, 1979.

Quinones, R. J. (1973). *The renaissance discovery of time.* Cambridge, MA: Harvard University Press.

Rank, O. (1936). *Will therapy.* New York: W. W. Norton, 1978.

Renvoize, J. (1978). *Web of violence.* London: Routledge & Kegan Paul.

Rifkin, J. (1987). *Time wars: the primary conflict in human history.* New York: Simon & Schuster.

Rochlin, G. (1973). *Man's aggression.* Boston, MA: Gambit.

Roe, A., & Simpson, G. G. (Eds.) (1958). *Behavior and evolution.* New Haven, CT: Yale University Press.

Rossi, P. (1984). *The dark abyss of time.* Chicago, IL: University of Chicago Press, 1994.

Rush, A. J. (Ed.) (1982). *Short-term psychotherapies for depression: behavioral, interpersonal, cognitive and psychodynamic approaches.* New York: John Wiley.

Russell, B. (1961). *Has man a future?* London: Allen & Unwin.

Russell, C., & Russell, W. M. S. (1968). *Violence, monkeys and man.* London: Macmillan.

Ryle, A. (1982). *Psychotherapy: a cognitive integration of theory and practice.* London: Academic Press.

Saul, L. J. (1972). *Psychodynamically based psychotherapy.* New York: Science House.

Schechter, D. E., Symonds, M., & Bernstein, I. (1955). The development of the concept of time in children. *Journal of Nervous and Mental Diseases, 121,* 301.

Schilder, P. (1936). Psychopathology of time. *Journal of Nervous and Mental Diseases, 83,* 530.

Schlosberg, A. (1969). Time perspective in schizophrenics. *Psychiatric Quarterly, 43,* 22–34.

Scott, J. P. (1958). *Aggression.* Chicago, IL: University of Chicago Press, 1976.

Scott, W. C. M. (1948). Some psycho-dynamic aspects of disturbed perception of time. *British Journal of Medical Psychology, 21,* 111.

Seinfeld, J. (1990). *The bad object: handling the negative therapeutic reaction in psychotherapy.* Northvale, NJ: Jason Aronson, 1993.

Shallis, M. (1982). *On time.* Harmondsworth: Pelican Books.

Sifneos, P. E. (1972). *Short-term psychotherapy and emotional crisis.* Cambridge, MA: Harvard University Press, 1978.

Sifneos, P. E. (1973). Confrontation in short-term anxiety-provoking psychotherapy. In: G. Adler & P. G. Myerson (Eds.), *Confrontation in psychotherapy* (pp. 369–383). New York: Science House.

Sifneos, P. E. (1978a). Evaluation criteria for selection of patients. In: H. Davanloo (Ed.), *Basic principles* (pp. 81–85). New York: Spectrum.

Sifneos, P. E. (1978b). Principles of technique in short-term anxiety-provoking psychotherapy. In: H. Davanloo (Ed.), *Basic principles* (pp. 329–332). New York: Spectrum.

Sifneos, P. E. (1978c). Short-term anxiety-provoking psychotherapy. In: H. Davanloo (Ed.), *Basic principles* (pp. 35–42). New York: Spectrum.

Sifneos, P. E. (1978d). Teaching and supervision of STAPP. In: H. Davanloo (Ed.), *Basic principles* (pp. 491–499). New York: Spectrum.

Sifneos, P. E. (1979). *Short-term dynamic psychotherapy: evaluation and technique.* New York & London: Plenum, 1983.

Sifneos, P. E. (1980a). Motivation for change. In: H. Davanloo (Ed.), *Short-term dynamic psychotherapy* (pp. 93–98). New York: Jason Aronson.

Sifneos, P. E. (1980b). Short-term anxiety-provoking psychotherapy. In: H. Davanloo (Ed.), *Short-term dynamic psychotherapy* (pp. 129–147). New York: Jason Aronson.

Sifneos, P. E. (1981). Short-term anxiety-provoking psychotherapy: its history, technique, outcome, and instructions. In: S. H. Budman (Ed.), *Forms of brief therapy* (pp. 45–81). New York: Guilford Press.

Small, L. (1971). *The briefer therapies.* New York: Brunner/ Mazel.

Smart, J. J. C. (1964). *Problems of space and time: a reader.* London: Collier Macmillan.

Staub, E. (1989). *The roots of evil: the origins of genocide and other group violence.* Cambridge: Cambridge University Press.

Stone, L. (1951). Psychoanalysis and brief psychotherapy. *Psychoanalytic Quarterly, 20,* 215.

Storr, A. (1968). *Human aggression.* Harmondsworth: Penguin.

Straker, M. (1978). Short-term dynamic psychotherapy: a retrospective and perspective view. In: H. Davanloo (Ed.), *Basic principles* (pp. 515–526). New York: Spectrum.

Straker, M. (1980). An overview. In: H. Davanloo (Ed.), *Short-term dynamic psychotherapy* (Part IV. Crisis intervention, pp. 221–236). New York: Jason Aronson.

Strupp, H. H. (1978). The challenge of short-term dynamic psychotherapy. In: H. Davanloo (Ed.), *Basic principles* (pp. 501–513). New York: Spectrum.

Strupp, H. H. (1980). Problems of research. In: H. Davanloo (Ed.), *Short-term dynamic psychotherapy* (pp. 379–392). New York: Jason Aronson.

Strupp, H. H. (1981). Toward the refinement of time-limited dynamic psychotherapy. In: S. H. Budman (Ed.), *Forms of brief therapy* (pp. 219–242). New York: Guilford Press.

Tinbergen, N. (1951). *The study of instinct.* Oxford: Oxford University Press, 1989.

Tinbergen, N. (1953). *Social behaviour in animals.* London: Chapman & Hale, 1990.

Toulmin, S., & Goodfield, J. (1961). *The discovery of time.* Chicago, IL: University of Chicago Press, 1982.

Trivers, H. (1985). *The rhythm of being: a study of temporality.* New York: Philosophical Library.

Trompf, G. W. (1979). *The idea of historical recurrence in Western thought.* Berkeley, CA: University of California Press.

Van der Kolk, B. A. (Ed.) (1987). *Psychological trauma.* Washington, DC: American Psychiatric Press.

Varma, V. (Ed.) (1974). *Psychotherapy today.* London: Constable.

Waal, F. de (1989). *Peacemaking among primates.* Cambridge, MA: Harvard University Press.

Wachtel, P. L. (1988). Foreword. In: S. H. Budman & A. S. Gurman (1988). *Theory and practice of brief therapy* (pp. vii–viii). London: Hutchinson.

Wahl, O., & Sieg, D. (1980). Time estimation among schizophrenics. *Perceptual and Motor Skills, 50,* 535.

Wallis, R. (1966). *Le temps, quatrième dimension de l'esprit.* Paris: Flammarion.

Washburn, S. L. (Ed.) (1961). *The social life of early man.* New York: Wenner-Gren Foundation for Anthropological Research.

Weisman, A. (1973). Confrontation, countertransference, and context. In: G. Adler & P. G. Myerson (Eds.), *Confrontation in psychotherapy* (pp. 97–121). New York: Science House.

Welpton, D. F. (1973). Confrontation in the therapeutic process. In: G. Adler & P. G. Myerson (Eds.), *Confrontation in psychotherapy* (pp. 249–269). New York: Science House.

Wendorff, R. (1980). *Zeit und Kultur: Geschichte des Zeitbewusstseins in Europa*. Wiesbaden: Westdeutscher Verlag.

Wessmann, A. E., & Gorman, B. S. (1977). *The personal experience of time*. New York: Plenum Press.

West, D. J. (1965). *Murder followed by suicide*. London: Heinemann.

White, H. S., Burke, J. D., Jr., & Havens, L. L. (1981). Choosing a method of short-term therapy: a developmental approach. In: S. H. Budman (Ed.), *Forms of brief therapy* (pp. 243–267). New York: Guilford Press.

Whitrow, G. J. (1961). *The natural philosophy of time*. London & Edinburgh: Nelson, 1980.

Whitrow, G. J. (1972). *What is time?* London: Thames & Hudson.

Whitrow, G. J. (1988). *Time in history: the evolution of our general awareness of time and temporal perspective*. Oxford: Oxford University Press.

Wiggins, K. M. (1983). The patient's relation to time during the final minutes of a psychotherapy session. *American Journal of Psychotherapy, 37* (1), 62–68.

Wilson, E. O. (1978). *On human nature*. Cambridge, MA: Harvard University Press.

Wilson, S. (1995). *The cradle of violence*. London: Jessica Kingsley Publishers.

Wilson, G. T. (1981). Behavior therapy as a short-term therapeutic approach. In: S. H. Budman (Ed.), *Forms of brief therapy* (pp. 131–166). New York: Guilford Press.

Winnicott, D. W. (1957). *The child, the family and the outside world*. Penguin Books, 1987.

Winnicott, D. W. (1958). *Through paediatrics to psycho-analysis*. With an introduction by M. Masud R. Khan. London: The Hogarth Press, 1977.

Winnicott, D. W. (1965). *The maturational processes and the facilitating environment: studies in the theory of emotional development*. London: The Hogarth Press, 1976.

Winnicott, D. W. (1971). *Playing and reality*. Harmondsworth: Penguin Books, 1974.

Winokur, M., Messer, S. B., & Schacht, T. (1981). Contributions to the theory and practice of short-term dynamic psychotherapy. *Bulletin of the Menninger Clinic, 45* (2), 125–142.

Wolberg, L. R. (1977). *The technique of psychotherapy.* New York: Grune & Stratton.

Wolberg, L. R. (1980). *Handbook of short-term psychotherapy.* New York: Thieme-Stratton.

Wudel, P. (1979). Time estimation and personality dimension. *Perceptual and Motor Skills, 48,* 1320.

Yates, A. J. (1962). *Frustration and conflict.* Westport, CT: Greenwood Press, 1982.

Young, M. (1988). *The metronomic society: natural rhythms and human timetables.* London: Thames & Hudson.

Yung, C. (1978). Research strategies in short-term dynamic psychotherapy. In: H. Davanloo (Ed.), *Basic principles* (pp. 527–549). New York: Spectrum.

Yung, C., & Davanloo, H. (1978). Where does evaluation end and therapy and techniques in short-term dynamic psychotherapy, begin? In: H. Davanloo (Ed.), *Basic principles* (pp. 291–306). New York: Spectrum.

Zahn-Waxler, C., Cummings, E. M., & Ianotti, R. (Eds.) (1984). *Social and biological origins of altruism and aggression.* Cambridge: Cambridge University Press, 1993.

Zerubavel, E. (1979). *Patterns of time in hospital life.* Chicago, IL: University of Chicago Press.

Zinberg, N. E. (1973). The technique of confrontation and social class difference. In: G. Adler & P. G. Myerson (Eds.), *Confrontation in psychotherapy* (pp. 271–301). New York: Science House.

Zulueta, F. de (1993). *From pain to violence: the traumatic roots of destructiveness.* London: Whurr Publishers.

# INDEX

A: *see* anxiety
abandonment:
  as focal theme, 42, 44
  threat of, 44, 86
absent parent 74
  (Example 8), 33–34
abstinence, 27, 30, 90
abuse:
  in families, 54
  of power, 78
  in school (Example 8), 33–34
acceptance of past, 90
accident-proneness, 57
acknowledgements, xvii
acting out:
  against boundaries
    (Examples 3, 4), 28
    (Example 5), 29
  as defence, 73
  and destructive anger, 57–58,
    62
  in session, 29
  against therapy, 62

active therapist, 42, 43
  needed for BDP, 39, 62
"active therapy" [Ferenczi], 13
addiction:
  to drugs, 9, 58
  to long-term therapy, xii, 20
  to timelessness, 20
administrative work, more in
    BDP, 14, 17
advice-giving, 85
affect, rapid shifts in, 73
affection, behind "wall", 74–75
aggression:
  and activity, 54
  constructive [Malan], 66
"aggressive" therapist, 10, 51–
    52
AIDS [acquired immune-
    deficiency syndrome]: *see*
    HIV/AIDS
aim(s), 77–92
  antitherapeutic, 85
  avoiding question of, 81